1000
THINGS
YOU SHOULD KNOW ABOUT

HUMAN BODY

Loretta K. Clinton

HUMAN BODY

John Farndon

Miles Kelly
PUBLISHING

**This edition first published in 2003 for
Books are Fun**

First published in 2000 by
Miles Kelly Publishing,
Bardfield Centre, Great Bardfield, Essex, CM7 4SL, U.K.
Copyright © Miles Kelly Publishing 2000, 2003

2 4 6 8 10 9 7 5 3 1

Library of Congress Cataloging-in-Publication Data on file
at the Library of Congress

ISBN 1-902947-30-4

Editorial Director: Anne Marshall
Editors: Amanda Learmonth, Jenni Rainford
Assistant: Liberty Newton
Americanization: Cindy Leaney
Written and designed by: John Farndon and Angela Koo

Printed in China

CONTENTS

KEY

 Breathing and blood

 Skeleton and muscle

 Body control

 Food and water

 Growing and changing

 Health and disease

Airways

- **The upper airways** include the nose and the sinuses, the mouth, and the pharynx (throat).

- **The lower airways** include the larynx (see vocal cords), the trachea (windpipe), and the airways of the lungs.

- **The sinuses** are air chambers within the bones of the skull that form the forehead and face. When blocked with mucus if you get a cold, your speech is affected.

- **The soft palate** is a flap of tissue at the back of the mouth, which is pressed upward when you swallow to stop food getting into your nose.

- **Your throat** is the tube that runs down through your neck from the back of your nose and mouth.

- **Your throat branches** in two at the bottom. One branch, the esophagus, takes food to the stomach. The other, the larynx, takes air to the lungs.

- **The epiglottis** is the flap that tilts down to block off the larynx to stop food entering it when you swallow.

- **The tonsils and the adenoids** are bunches of lymph nodes (see lymphatic system) that swell to help fight ear, nose, and throat infections, especially in young children.

- **The adenoids** are at the back of the nose, and the tonsils are at the back of the upper throat.

- **If tonsils or adenoids** swell too much, they are sometimes taken out.

Lungs

◄ *The lower airways include the larynx, the trachea (windpipe), and the bronchi which branch into the lungs.*

> ★ STAR FACT ★
> Your throat is linked to your ears by tubes which open when you swallow to balance air pressure.

Smell

▲ *Scents are closely linked to emotions in the brain, and perfume can be a powerful way of triggering feelings.*

- **Smells are scent molecules** which are carried in the air and breathed in up your nose. A particular smell may be noticeable even when just a single scent molecule is mixed in with millions of air molecules.

- **The human nose** can tell the difference between more than 10,000 different chemicals.

- **Dogs can pick up** smells that are 10,000 times fainter than the ones humans can detect.

- **Inside the nose**, scent molecules are picked up by a patch of cells called the olfactory epithelium.

- **Olfactory** means "to do with the sense of smell."

- **The olfactory epithelium** contains over 25 million receptor cells.

- **Each of the receptor cells** in the olfactory epithelium has up to 20 or so scent-detecting hairs called cilia.

- **When they are triggered** by scent molecules, the cilia send signals to a cluster of nerves called the olfactory bulb, which then sends messages to the part of the brain that recognizes smell.

- **The part of the brain** that deals with smell is closely linked to the parts that deal with memories and emotions. This may be why smells can evoke memories.

- **By the age of 20**, you will have lost 20 percent of your sense of smell. By 60, you will have lost 60 percent of it.

Central nervous system

- **The central nervous system** (CNS) is made up of the brain and the spinal cord (the nerves of the spine).

- **The CNS** contains billions of densely packed interneurons—nerve cells with very short connecting axons (see nerve cells).

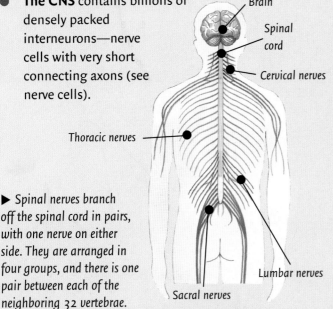

Brain

Spinal cord

Cervical nerves

Thoracic nerves

Lumbar nerves

Sacral nerves

▶ *Spinal nerves branch off the spinal cord in pairs, with one nerve on either side. They are arranged in four groups, and there is one pair between each of the neighboring 32 vertebrae.*

- **The CNS is cushioned** from damage by a surrounding bath of cerebrospinal fluid.

- **There are 86 main nerves** branching off the CNS. These consist of 12 pairs of cranial nerves and 31 pairs of spinal nerves (43 pairs).

- **Cranial nerves** are the 12 pairs of nerves that branch off the CNS in the head.

- **Spinal nerves** are the 31 pairs of nerves that branch off the spinal cord.

- **The spinal nerves** are made up of 8 cervical nerve pairs, 12 thoracic pairs, 5 lumbar pairs, 5 sacral pairs, and 1 coccyx pair.

- **Many spinal nerves** join up just outside the spine in five junctions called plexuses.

> ★ **STAR FACT** ★
> The CNS sends out messages to more than 640 muscles around the body.

Carbohydrates

- **Carbohydrates** in food are your body's main source of energy. They are plentiful in sweet things and in starchy food such as bread, cake, and potatoes (see Diet).

- **Carbohydrates** are burned by the body to keep it warm and to provide energy for growth and muscle movement, as well as to maintain basic body processes.

- **Carbohydrates** are among the most common of all organic (life) substances. Plants, for instance, make carbohydrates when they take energy from sunlight.

- **Carbohydrates** include huge molecules made of long strings of smaller chemical substances called sugars. Sucrose (the sugar in sugar cubes and granulated sugar) is just one of these sugars.

- **Simple carbohydrates** such as glucose, fructose (the sweetness in fruit), and sucrose are sweet and soluble (they will dissolve in water).

- **Complex carbohydrates** (or polysaccharides) such as starch are joined molecules of simple carbohydrates.

- **A third type of carbohydrate** is cellulose (see Diet).

- **The carbohydrates** you eat are turned into glucose for your body to use at once, or stored in the liver as the complex sugar glycogen (body starch).

- **The average adult** needs 2,000 to 4,000 kilojoules (Calories) of carbohydrate a day.

- **A Calorie** is the heat needed to warm 2pt (1l) of water by 1°C.

▼ *Bread is especially rich in complex carbohydrates such as starch, as well as simpler ones such as glucose and sucrose. Both were made by the original cereal plant whose seeds were ground into flour.*

Veins

- **Veins** are pipes in the body for carrying blood back to the heart.

- **Unlike arteries**, most veins carry "used" blood back to the heart—the body cells have taken the oxygen they need from the blood, so it is low in oxygen.

- **When blood** is low in oxygen, it is a dark, purplish-blue color—unlike the bright red of the oxygenated blood carried by the arteries.

- **The only veins** that carry oxygenated blood are the four pulmonary veins, which carry blood from the lungs the short distance to the heart.

- **The two largest veins** in the body are the vena cavae that flow into the heart from above and below.

- **Inside most large veins** are flaps that act as valves to

> ★ STAR FACT ★
> At any moment 75 percent (three-quarters)
> of the body's blood is in veins.

make sure that the blood only flows one way.

- **The blood in veins** (as with the arteries) is pumped by the heart, but the blood pressure in veins is much lower than in arteries and vein walls do not need to be as strong.

- **Unlike arteries**, veins collapse when empty.

- **Blood is helped through** the veins by pressure placed on the vein walls by the surrounding muscles.

▶ *The main veins in the lower arm are in blue, the main arteries in red.*

Basilic vein

Ulnar artery

Radial artery

Teeth

▼ *Teeth have long roots that slot into sockets in the jawbones, but they sit in a fleshy ridge called the gums. In the center of each tooth is a living pulp of blood and nerves. Around this is a layer of dentine, then on top of that a tough shield of enamel.*

Molar surface

Coating of enamel

Gum

Soft core or pulp

Dentine layer

Jawbone   Root canal

- **Milk teeth** are the 20 teeth that start to appear when a baby is about six months old.

- **When you are six**, you start to grow your 32 adult teeth: 16 top in the top row and 16 in the bottom.

- **Molars** are the (usually) six pairs of big, strong teeth at the back of your mouth. They have flattish tops and are a good shape for grinding food.

- **The rearmost four molars**, one in each back corner of each jaw, are the wisdom teeth. These are the last to grow and sometimes they never appear.

- **Premolars** are four pairs of teeth in front of the molars.

- **Incisors** are the four pairs of teeth at the front of your mouth. They have sharp edges for cutting food.

- **Canines** are the two pairs of big, pointed teeth behind the incisors. Their shape is good for tearing food.

- **The enamel** on teeth is the body's hardest substance.

- **Dentine** inside teeth is softer but still hard as bone.

The thyroid gland

- **The thyroid** is a small gland about the size of two joined cherries. It is at the front of your neck, just below the larynx (see Airways and The vocal cords).

- **The thyroid** secretes (releases) three important hormones: tri-iodothyronine (T3), thyroxine (T4), and calcitonin.

- **The thyroid hormones** affecct how energetic you are by controlling your metabolic rate.

- **Your metabolic rate** is the rate at which your body cells use glucose, and other substances.

▶ The thyroid is part of your energy control system, telling your body cells to work faster or slower in order to keep you warm or to make your muscles work harder.

- **T3 and T4** control metabolic rate by circulating into the blood and stimulating cells to convert more glucose.

- **If the thyroid** sends out too little T3 and T4, you get cold and tired, your skin gets dry, and you put on weight.

- **If the thyroid** sends out too much T3 and T4, you get nervous, sweaty, and overactive, and you lose weight.

- **The amount of T3 and T4** sent out by the thyroid depends on how much thyroid-stimulating hormone is sent to it from the pituitary gland (see The brain).

- **If the levels of T3 and T4** in the blood drop, the pituitary gland sends out extra thyroid-stimulating hormone to tell the thyroid to produce more.

Water

- **Your body** is mainly made of water—over 60 percent.

- **You can survive weeks** without food, but no more than a few days without water.

- **You gain water** by drinking and eating, and as a by-product of cell activity.

- **You lose water** by sweating and breathing, and in your urine and feces (see Excretion).

- **The average person** takes in 4.6pt (2.2l) of water a day: 3pt (1.4l) in drink and 1.7pt (0.8l) in food. Body cells add 0.6pt (0.3l), bringing the total water intake to 5.2pt (2.5l).

- **The average person** loses 3.2pt (1.5l) of water every day in urine, 1pt (0.5l) in sweat, 0.6pt (0.3l) as vapor in the breath, and 0.4pt (0.2l) in feces.

- **The water balance** in the body is controlled mainly by the kidneys and adrenal glands.

- **The amount of water** the kidneys let out as urine depends on the amount of salt there is in the blood (see Body salts).

▶ If you sweat a lot during heavy exercise, you need to make up for all the water you have lost by drinking. Your kidneys make sure that if you drink too much, you lose water as urine.

- **If you drink a lot,** the saltiness of the blood is diluted (watered down). To restore the balance, the kidneys let out a lot of water in the form of urine.

- **If you drink little** or sweat a lot, the blood becomes more salty, so the kidneys restore the balance by holding on to more water.

Diet

◀ Garlic may give you fairly unpleasant breath and make your skin smell, but it is supposed to be good for the heart.

- **Your diet** is what you eat. A good diet includes the correct amount of proteins, carbohydrates, fats, vitamins, minerals, fiber and water.

- **Most of the food** you eat is fuel for the body, provided mostly by carbohydrates and fats.

- **Carbohydrates** are foods made from kinds of sugar, such as glucose and starch. They are found in foods such as bread, rice, potatoes, and sweet things.

- **Fats** are greasy foods that will not dissolve in water. Some, such as the fats in meat and cheese, are solid. Some, such as cooking oil, are liquid.

- **Fats are not** usually burned up right away, but stored around your body until they are needed.

- **Proteins** are needed to build and repair cells, and they are made from chemicals called amino acids.

- **There are 20** different amino acids—your body can make 11 of them. The other nine are called essential acids and they come from food.

- **Meat and fish** are very high in protein.

- **A correctly balanced vegetarian diet** of eggs, milk, and cheese can provide all the essential amino acids.

- **Fiber** or roughage is supplied by cellulose from plant cell walls. Your body cannot digest fiber, but needs it to exercise the bowel muscles.

▶ Citrus fruits are a good source of vitamin C, which is vital for healthy teeth, gums and bones.

Babies

◀ Babies start to crawl when their leg muscles grow strong enough, after nine months or so.

- **A baby's head** is three-quarters of the size it will be as an adult, and a quarter of its total body height.

- **The bones** of a baby's skeleton are fairly soft, to allow for growth. They harden over time.

- **Baby boys grow faster** than baby girls during the first seven months.

- **A baby** has a very developed sense of taste, with taste buds all over the inside of its mouth.

- **Babies have** a much stronger sense of smell than adults—perhaps to help them find their mother.

- **There are two gaps** called fontanelles between the bones of a baby's skull, where there is only membrane (a "skin" of thin tissue), not bone. The gaps close and the bones join together by about 18 months.

- **A baby is born** with primitive reflexes (things it does automatically) such as grasping or sucking a finger.

- **A baby's bodyweight** actually triples in the first year of its life.

- **A baby seems to learn** to control its body in stages, starting first with its head, then moving on to its arms and legs.

> ★ STAR FACT ★
> A baby's brain is one of the fastest growing parts of its body.

The brain

- **The human brain** is made up of more than 100 billion nerve cells called neurons.

- **Each neuron** is connected to as many as 25,000 other neurons, so the brain has trillions and trillions of different pathways for nerve signals.

- **Girls' brains** weigh 2.5 percent of their body weight, on average, while boys' brains weigh 2 percent.

- **About 1.5pt** (0.8l) of blood shoots through your brain every minute. The brain may be just 2 percent of your body weight, demanding 12–15 percent of your blood supply.

- **An elephant's brain** weighs four times as much as the human brain. Some apes, monkeys, and dolphins are quite near our brain-body ratio.

- **The cerebral cortex**, the outside of the upper part of the brain, would cover a bed if it was laid out flat.

- **The left hemisphere (half)** of the brain is more dominant in speech, writing, and general language, the right half in pictures and ideas.

> **! NEWS FLASH !**
> Scientists can now grow human
> brain cells in a laboratory dish.

- **Conscious thoughts and actions** happen in the cerebral cortex.

- **A human brain** has a cerebral cortex four times as big as a chimpanzee, about 20 times as big as a monkey's, and about 300 times as big as a rat's.

- **Unconscious, automatic activities** such as breathing, hunger, sleep, and so on are controlled by structures such as the hypothalamus and the hippocampus in the middle of the brain.

- **The cerebellum** mainly controls body co-ordination and balance.

Cerebrum, where you think and decide what to say and other clever things

Hypothalamus controls body heat, water, and hunger, and also wakes you up

Thalamus affects sensory levels, awareness and alertness

Limbic system affects body functions, emotions, and smell

Pituitary gland controls hormones

Hippocampus, linked to moods, willpower, learning, and memory

Amygdala, llinked to moods and memories

Cerebellum controls coordination

Brain stem controls heartbeat and breathing

▲ The right hemisphere (half) of the cerebrum is shown in pink, surrounding the regions that control basic drives such as hunger, thirst, and anger.

▼ Taking the top off the skull shows the brain to be a soggy, pinkish-gray mass which looks sort of like a giant walnut.

Tendons and ligaments

- **Tendons** are cords that tie a muscle to a bone or a muscle to another muscle.

- **Most tendons** are round, rope-like bundles of fiber. A few, such as the ones in the abdomen wall, are flat sheets called aponeuroses.

- **Tendon fibers are made** from a rubbery substance called collagen.

- **Your fingers are moved** mainly by muscles in the forearm, connected to the fingers by long tendons.

- **The Achilles tendon** pulls up your heel at the back.

- **Ligaments** are cords attached to bones on either side of a joint. They strengthen the joint.

- **Ligaments** also support various organs, including the liver, bladder, and uterus (womb).

> ★ STAR FACT ★
> The Achilles tendon is named after the Greek hero Achilles whose only weakness was his heel.

- **Women's breasts** are held in shape by bundles of ligaments.

- **Ligaments are made up** of bundles of tough collagen and a stretchy substance called elastin.

▶ Collateral (side) ligaments stop the knee wobbling from side to side. Cruciate (crossing) ligaments tie the knee across the middle to stop it bending or straightening too much. Tendons hold the kneecap in place.

Kneecap (patella)

Cruciate ligaments

Collateral ligaments

Vaccination

- **Vaccination** helps to protect you against an infectious disease by exposing you to a mild or dead version of the germ in order to make your body build up protection, in the form of antibodies.

- **Vaccination** is also called immunization, because it builds up your resistance or immunity to a disease.

- **In passive immunization** you are injected with substances such as antibodies which have already been exposed to the germ and developed antibodies.

◀ Diseases such as diphtheria, rubella, and whooping cough are now rare in many countries thanks to vaccination. The dangerous disease smallpox—once very common—has been wiped out.

- **In active immunization** you are given a killed or otherwise harmless version of the germ. Your body makes the antibodies itself for long-term protection.

- **Children in many countries** are given a series of vaccinations as they grow up, to protect them against diseases such as diphtheria, tetanus, and polio.

- **There is a small risk** of a serious reaction against a vaccine. The measles vaccine carries a 1 in 87,000 chance of causing encephalitis (brain inflammation).

- **In cholera, typhoid, rabies, and flu vaccines**, the germ in the vaccine is killed to make it harmless.

- **In measles, mumps, polio, and rubella vaccines**, the germ is live attenuated—this means that its genes or other parts have been altered to make it harmless.

- **In diphtheria and tetanus vaccines**, the germ's toxins (poisons) are removed to make them harmless.

- **The hepatitis B vaccine** can be prepared by genetic engineering.

Thinking

- **Some scientists** claim that we humans are the only living things that are conscious—we alone are actually aware that we are thinking.

- **No one knows** how consciousness works, it is one of science's last great mysteries.

- **Most thoughts** seem to take place in the cerebrum (at the top of your brain), and different kinds of thought are linked to different areas, called association areas.

▲ Modern scanning techniques have taught us a great deal about the human brain and brain processes by allowing us to see brains in action.

- **Each half of the cerebrum** has four rounded ends called lobes: two at the front (frontal and temporal lobes) and two at the back (occipital and parietal lobes).

- **The frontal lobe** is linked to your personality and it is where you have your bright ideas.

- **The temporal lobe** is where you hear and understand what people say to you.

- **The occipital lobe** is where you figure out what your eyes see.

- **The parietal lobe** is where you register touch, heat and cold, and pain.

- **The left half of the brain** (left hemisphere) controls the right side of the body. The right half (right hemisphere) controls the left side.

- **One half of the brain** is always dominant (in charge). Usually, the left brain is dominant, which is why 90 percent of people are right-handed.

Chromosomes

- **Chromosomes** are the microscopically tiny, twisted threads inside every cell that carry your body's life instructions in chemical form.

- **There are 46 chromosomes** in each of your body cells, divided into 23 pairs.

- **One of each chromosome pair** came from your mother and the other from your father

- **In a girl's 23 chromosome pairs**, each half exactly matches the other (the set from the mother is equivalent to the set from the father).

- **Boys** have 22 matching chromosome pairs, but the 23rd pair is made up of two odd chromosomes.

- **The 23rd chromosome pair** decides what sex you are, and the sex chromosomes are called X and Y.

- **Girls** have two X chromosomes, but boys have an X and a Y chromosome.

- **In every matching pair**, both chromosomes give your body life instructions for the same thing.

- **The chemical instructions** on each chromosome come in thousands of different units called genes.

- **Genes for the same feature** appear in the same place on each matching pair of chromosomes in human body cells. Scientists have now mapped almost the entire pattern, called the genome.

▼ Girls turn out to be girls because they get an X—not a Y—chromosome from their father.

Circulation

▶ Blood circulates round and round your body continuously through an intricate series of tubes called blood vessels. Bright red, oxygen-rich blood is pumped from the left side of the heart through vessels called arteries and arterioles. Purplish-blue, low-in-oxygen blood returns to the right of the heart through veins and venules.

The brain receives more blood than any other part of the body

Blood returns to the heart through main veins called the vena cavae

The pulmonary circulation takes blood to and from the lungs

Blood leaves the left side of the heart through a giant artery called the aorta

Radial artery

Iliac vein

Femoral artery

Saphenous vein

Peroneal artery

For each outward-going artery there is usually an equivalent returning vein

- **Your circulation** is the system of tubes called blood vessels which carries blood out from your heart to all your body cells and back again.

- **Blood circulation** was discovered in 1628 by the English physician William Harvey (1578–1657), who built on the ideas of Matteo Colombo.

- **Each of the body's** 600 billion cells gets fresh blood once every few minutes or less.

- **On the way out** from the heart, blood is pumped through vessels called arteries and arterioles.

> ★ STAR FACT ★
> It takes less than 90 seconds on average for blood to circulate through all of the body's 60,000mi (100,000km) of blood vessels!

- **On the way back** to the heart, blood flows through venules and veins.

- **Blood flows** from the arterioles to the venules through the tiniest tubes called capillaries.

- **The blood circulation** has two parts: the pulmonary and the systemic.

- **The pulmonary circulation** is the short section that carries blood which is low in oxygen from the right side of the heart to the lungs for "refuelling." It then returns oxygen-rich blood to the left side of the heart.

- **The systemic circulation** carries oxygen-rich blood from the left side of the heart all around the body, and returns blood which is low in oxygen to the right side of the heart.

- **Inside the blood**, oxygen is carried by the hemoglobin in red blood cells (see Blood cells).

◀ Red blood cells can actually be brown in color, but they turn bright scarlet when their hemoglobin is carrying oxygen. After the hemoglobin passes its oxygen to a cell, it fades to dull purple. So oxygen-rich blood from the heart is red, while oxygen-poor blood that is returning to the heart is a purplish-blue color.

Birth

- **Babies are usually born** 38-42 weeks after the mother becomes pregnant.

- **Usually, a few days or weeks before birth**, the baby turns so its head is pointing down toward the mother's birth canal (her cervix and vagina).

- **Birth begins** as the mother goes into labor, when the womb muscles begin a rhythm of contracting (tightening) and relaxing in order to push the baby out through the birth canal.

- **There are three stages** of labor. In the first, the womb muscles contract or squeeze, bursting the bag of fluid around the baby. This is called breaking the waters.

- **In the second stage** of labor, the baby is pushed out through the birth canal. Then the umbilical cord—its lifeline to its mother—is cut and the baby starts to breathe on its own.

- **In the third stage** of labor, the placenta is shed and comes out through the birth canal.

- **A premature baby** is one born before it is fully developed.

- **A miscarriage** is when the developing baby is "born" before the 28th week of pregnancy and cannot survive.

- **A Caesarian section** is an operation for when a baby cannot be born through the birth canal. It is delivered through a surgical cut in the mother's belly.

▼ *A mother makes a special bond with her baby.*

Diagnosis

▲ *To diagnose certain illnesses correctly, a doctor may need to carry out a number different tests.*

- **Diagnosis** is when a doctor figures out what illness or condition a patient has—and perhaps its cause.

- **The history** is the patient's own account of their illness. This provides the doctor with a lot of clues.

- **The prognosis** is the doctor's assessment of how the illness will develop in future.

- **Symptoms** are the effects or signs of the illness.

- **After taking a history** the doctor may carry out a physical examination, looking at the patient's body for symptoms such as swelling and tenderness.

- **A stethoscope** is a set of ear tubes which allows the doctor to listen to body sounds such as breathing and the heart beating.

- **With certain symptoms**, a doctor may order special tests, such as laboratory tests of blood and urine samples. Devices such as ultrasounds and X-rays may also be used to take special pictures.

- **Doctors** nowadays may use computers to help them make a diagnosis.

- **Diagnosis** can take a few seconds or many months.

> **! NEWS FLASH !**
> In future, many illnesses will be diagnosed entirely by computer.

The cortex

- **A cortex** is the outer layer of any organ, such as the brain or the kidney.

- **The brain's cortex** is also known as the cerebral cortex. It is a layer of interconnected nerve cells around the outside of the brain, called "gray matter."

- **The cerebral cortex** is where many signals from the senses are registered in the brain.

◀ The surface of the cortex is wrinkled into folds which are called gyri, with valleys in between them called sulci. The pattern of wrinkles can be seen clearly in this scan, which creates a slice through the brain.

- **The visual cortex** is around the lower back of the brain. It is the place where all the things you see are registered in the brain.

- **The somatosensory cortex** is a band running over the top of the brain like a headband. This where a touch on any part of the body is registered.

- **The motor cortex** is a band just in front of the sensory cortex. It sends out signals to body muscles to move.

- **The more nerve endings** there are in a particular part of the body, the more of the sensory cortex it occupies.

- **The lips and face** take up a huge proportion of the sensory cortex.

- **The hands** take up almost as much of the sensory cortex as the face.

> ★ STAR FACT ★
> Everyone has their own unique pattern of wrinkles on their cerebral cortex.

Bone

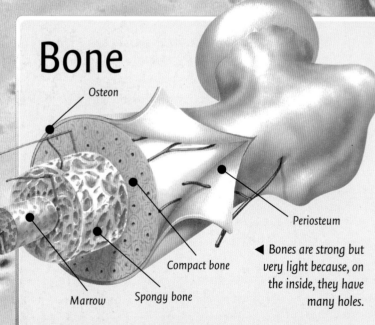

Osteon

Periosteum

Compact bone

Marrow   Spongy bone

◀ Bones are strong but very light because, on the inside, they have many holes.

- **Bones are so strong** that they can cope with twice the sqeezing pressure that granite can, or four times the stretching tension that concrete can, before breaking.

- **Weight for weight,** bone is at least five times as strong as steel.

- **Bones are so light** they only make up 14 percent of your body's total weight.

- **Bones get their rigidity** from hard deposits of minerals such as calcium and phosphate.

- **Bones get their flexibility** from tough, elastic, rope-like fibers of collagen.

- **The hard outside of bones** (called compact bone) is reinforced by strong rods called osteons.

- **The inside of bones** (called spongy bone) is a light honeycomb, made of thin struts or trabeculae, perfectly angled to take stress.

- **The core of some bones,** such as the long bones in an arm or leg, is called bone marrow. It is soft and jello-like.

- **In some parts of each bone,** there are special cells called osteoblasts which make new bone. In other parts, cells called osteoclasts break up old bone.

- **Bones grow** by getting longer near the end—at a region called the epiphyseal plate.

The spinal cord

- **The spinal cord** is the bundle of nerves running down the middle of the backbone.

- **The spinal cord** is the route for all nerve signals traveling between the brain and the body.

- **The spinal cord** can actually work independently of the brain, sending out responses to the muscles.

- **The outside** of the spinal cord is made of the long tails or axons of nerve cells and is called white matter; the inside is made of the main nerve bodies and is called gray matter.

- **Your spinal cord** is about 17in (43cm) long and 0.4in (1cm) thick; it stops growing when you are about five years old.

- **Damage to the spinal cord** can cause paralysis.

- **Injuries below the neck** can cause paraplegia— paralysis below the waist.

- **Injuries to the neck** can cause quadraplegia— paralysis below the neck.

- **Descending pathways** are groups of nerves that carry nerve signals down the spinal cord— typically signals from the brain for muscles to move.

- **Ascending pathways** are groups of nerves that carry nerve signals up the spinal cord— typically signals from the skin and internal body sensors going to the brain.

Nerve root

Spinal nerve

Vertebra (single backbone)

Disk between two vertebrae

▶ The spinal cord is encased in a tunnel in the backbone at the back of each vertebra. Nerves branch off to the body in pairs either side.

Vitamins

- **Vitamins** are special substances the body needs to help maintain chemical processes inside cells.

- **Plants can make** their own vitamins, but humans must take most of their own from food.

- **A lack of any vitamin** in the diet can cause illness.

- **Before the 18th century,** sailors on long voyages used to get the disease scurvy, caused by a lack of vitamin C from fresh fruit in their diet.

- **There are at least 15 vitamins** known.

- **The first vitamins** discovered were given letter names like B. Later discoveries were given chemical names.

- **Some vitamins** such as A, D, E, and K dissolve in fat and are found in animal fats and vegetable oils. They may be stored in the body for months.

- **Some vitamins** such as C and the Bs, dissolve in water and are found in green leaves, fruits, and cereal grains. They are used daily.

★ STAR FACT ★
Lack of vitamin A ruins night vision, because it is needed for the working of the retina.

- **Vitamins D and K** are the only ones made in the body. Vitamin D is essential for bone growth in children. It is made by the skin when exposed to the sun—15 minutes three times a week may be enough.

▶ This is a microscope photograph of a crystal of vitamin C, also known as ascorbic acid. This vitamin helps the body fight infections such as colds.

Disease

- **A disease** is something that upsets the normal working of any living thing. It can be acute (sudden, but short-lived), chronic (long-lasting), malignant (spreading), or benign (not spreading).

- **Some diseases** are classified by the body part they affect (such as heart disease), or by the body activity they affect (such as respiratory, or breathing, disease).

- **Heart disease** is the most common cause of death in the United States, Europe, and Australia.

- **Some diseases** are classified by their cause. These include the diseases caused by the staphylococcus bacteria, such as pneumonia.

- **Diseases can be** either contagious (able to be passed on) or non-infectious.

- **Infectious diseases** are caused by germs such as

◀ *This is a microscope photograph of a cancer cell.*

bacteria and viruses (see Germs). They include the common cold, polio, flu, and measles. Their spread can be controlled by good sanitation and hygiene, and by vaccination programs.

- **Non-infectious diseases** may be inherited or they may be caused by such things as eating harmful substances, poor nutrition or hygiene, getting old, or being injured.

- **Endemic diseases** are diseases that occur in a particular area of the world, such as sleeping sickness in Africa.

- **Cancer** is a disease in which malignant cells multiply abnormally, creating growths called tumors.

- **Cancer kills** 6 million people a year around the world. The risk increases as you get older.

Blood groups

◀ *Lives often depend on a patient receiving blood donated by someone else. But unless the blood belongs to a suitable donor, the patient's body will react against it.*

- **Around 85 percent of people** are Rh+. The remaining 15 percent are Rh−.

- **If your blood is Rh+** and your group is A, your blood group is said to be A positive. If your blood is Rh− and your group is O, you are O negative, and so on.

- **The Rhesus factors** got their name because they were first identified in Rhesus monkeys.

- **A transfusion** is when you are given blood from another person's body. Your blood is "matched" with other blood considered safe for transfusion.

- **Blood transfusions** are given when someone has lost too much blood because of an injury or operation. It is also given to replace diseased blood.

- **Most people's blood** belongs to one of four groups or types: A, O, B, and AB.

- **Blood type O** is the most common, followed by type A.

- **Blood is also** either Rhesus positive (Rh+) or Rhesus negative (Rh−).

★ STAR FACT ★
A pregnant mother who is Rh− may develop damaging antibodies against the baby in her own womb if it is Rh+.

Digestion

- **Digestion** is the process by which your body breaks down the food you eat into substances that it can absorb (take in) and use.

- **Your digestive tract** is basically a long, winding tube called the alimentary canal (gut). It starts at your mouth and ends at your anus.

- **If you could lay** your gut out straight, it would be nearly six times as long as you are tall.

- **The food you eat** is softened in your mouth by chewing and by chemicals in your saliva (spit).

- **When you swallow**, food travels down your esophagus (gullet) into your stomach. Your stomach is a muscular-walled bag which mashes the food into a pulp, helped by chemicals called gastric juices.

- **When empty**, your stomach holds barely 1pt (0.5l), but after a meal it can stretch to more than 8pt (4l).

- **The half-digested food** that leaves your stomach is called chyme. It passes into your small intestine.

- **Your small intestine** is a 20ft (6m) long tube where chyme is broken down further, into molecules that are absorbed through the intestine wall into the blood.

- **Food that cannot be** digested in your small intestine passes on into your large intestine. It is then pushed out through your anus as feces when you go to the toilet (see Excretion).

- **Digestive enzymes** play a vital part in breaking food down so it can be absorbed by the body.

▼ The food you eat is broken down into the nutrients your body needs as it passes down through your esophagus into your stomach and your small intestine. Undigested food travels through your large intestine and leaves your body via your anus.

◄ Food is moved through your digestive system by the muscles of the gut wall contracting (tightening) and relaxing. This rippling movement is called peristalsis. Whenever food enters the gut, rings of muscle contract behind it, while muscles in front relax, easing the food slowly forward.

▶ The small intestine is lined with tiny, finger-like folds called villi. On the surface of each villi are even tinier, finger-like folds called microvilli. These folds give a huge area for absorbing food.

Salivary glands make saliva

Food swallowed goes down the esophagus (gullet)

Liver plays a vital role in processing digested food

Pancreas secretes digestive juices

Stomach secretes gastric acids and enzymes

Small intestine

Large intestine

Appendix

Rectum

Anus

★ STAR FACT ★
On average, food takes 24 hours to pass all the way through your alimentary canal and out the other end.

Joints

- **Body joints** are places where bones meet.

- **The skull** is not one bone, but 22 separate bones bound tightly together with fibers so that they cannot move.

- **Most body joints** (apart from fixed joints like the skull's fibrous joints) let bones move, but different kinds of joint let them move in different ways.

- **Hinge joints**, such as the elbow, let the bones swing to and fro in two directions like door hinges do.

- **In ball-and-socket joints**, such as the shoulder and hip, the rounded end of one bone sits in the cup-shaped socket of the other and can move in almost any direction.

- **Swivel joints** turn like a wheel on an axle. Your head can swivel to the left or to the right on your spine.

> ★ STAR FACT ★
> The knee joint can bend, straighten, and
> (when slightly bent) rotate.

- **Saddle joints** such as those in the thumb have the bones interlocking like two saddles. These joints allow great mobility with considerable strength.

- **The relatively inflexible** joints between the bones (vertebrae) of the spine are cushioned by pads of cartilage.

- **Synovial joints** are flexible joints such as the hip-joint, lubricated with oily "synovial fluid" and cushioned by cartilage.

Synovial fluid
Ligaments and synovial sheath
Hip bone
Cartilage
Thigh bone

▶ *The hip joint is a ball-and-socket joint which takes a great deal of wear and tear. When the cushioning layer of cartilage breaks down, it can be replaced with an artificial joint made of special plastics.*

Nerve cells

- **Nerves** are made of special cells: neurons.

- **Neurons** are spider-shaped with a nucleus at the center, branching threads—dendrites —and a winding tail called an axon which can be up to 3ft (1m) long.

- **Axon terminals** on the axons of one neuron link to the dendrites or cell body of another neuron.

- **Neurons link** like beads on a string to make your nervous system.

▲ *Microscopically tiny nerve cells like this were first seen by being stained with silver nitrate by the Italian scientist Camillo Golgi in the 1870s.*

- **Most cells are** short-lived and are constantly replaced by new ones. Neurons, however, are long-lived—some are never replaced after you are born.

- **Nerve signals** travel as electrical pulses, each pulse lasting about 0.001 seconds.

- **When nerves are resting** there are extra sodium ions with a positive electrical charge on the outside of the nerve cell.

- **When a nerve fires**, little gates open in the cell wall all along the nerve, and positive ions rush in to join the negative ions.

- **Long-distance nerves** are insulated (covered) by a sheath of myelin to keep the signal strong.

- **Myelinated (myelin-sheathed) nerves** shoot signals through very fast—at about 300ft/sec (100m/sec).

- **Ordinary nerves** send signals at about 3 to 6ft /sec (1 to 2m/sec).

The lungs

- **Your lungs** are a pair of soft, spongy bags inside your chest.

- **When you breathe** in, air rushes in through your nose or mouth, down your trachea (windpipe), and into the hundreds of branching airways in your lungs.

- **The two biggest airways** are called bronchi, and they both branch into smaller airways called bronchioles.

▲ Taken through a powerful microscope, this photo of a slice of lung tissue shows a blood vessel and the very thin walls of an alveolus next to it.

- **The surface of your airways** is protected by a slimy film of mucus, which gets thicker to protect the lungs when you have a cold.

- **At the end of each bronchiole** are bunches of minute air sacs called alveoli (singular alveolus).

- **Alveoli** are wrapped around with tiny blood vessels, and alveoli walls are just one cell thick—thin enough to let oxygen and carbon dioxide seep through them.

- **There are 300 million alveoli** in your lungs.

- **The huge surface area** of all these alveoli makes it possible for huge quantities of oxygen to seep through into the blood. Equally huge quantities of carbon dioxide can seep back into the airways for removal when you breathe out.

> ★ STAR FACT ★
> Opened out and laid flat, the alveoli would cover half a football field.

The liver

- **The liver** is your chemical processing center.

- **The liver is your body's biggest internal organ**, and the word hepatic means "to do with the liver."

- **The liver's prime task** is handling all the nutrients and substances digested from the food you eat and sending them out to your body cells when needed.

- **The liver turns** carbohydrates into glucose, the main energy-giving chemical for body cells.

- **The liver keeps** the levels of glucose in the blood steady. It does this by releasing more when levels drop, and by storing it as glycogen, a type of starch, when levels rise.

- **The liver packs off** any excess food energy to be stored as fat around the body.

- **The liver breaks down** proteins and stores vitamins and minerals.

- **The liver produces bile**, the yellowish or greenish bitter liquid that helps dissolve fat as food is digested.

- **The liver clears the blood** of old red cells and harmful substances such as alcohol, and makes new plasma (see Blood).

- **The liver's chemical processing units** are thousands of hexagonal-shaped units called lobules. These take in unprocessed blood on the outside and dispatch it through a collecting vein in the center of each.

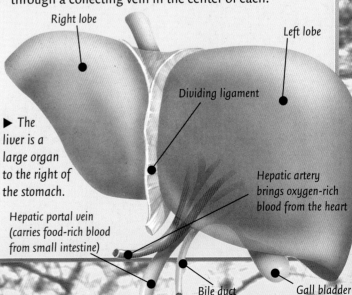

▶ The liver is a large organ to the right of the stomach.

Right lobe

Left lobe

Dividing ligament

Hepatic artery brings oxygen-rich blood from the heart

Hepatic portal vein (carries food-rich blood from small intestine)

Bile duct

Gall bladder

Genes

- **Genes** are the body's chemical instructions for your entire life—for growing up, surviving, having children, and, perhaps, even for dying.

- **Individual genes** are instructions to make particular proteins—the body's building-block molecules.

- **Small sets of genes** control features such as the color of your hair or your eyes, or create a particular body process such as digesting fat from food.

- **Each of your body cells** (except egg and sperm cells) carries identical sets of genes. This is because all your cells were made by other cells splitting in two, starting with the original egg cell in your mother.

- **Your genes are a mixture**—half come from your mother and half from your father (see Chromosomes). But none of your brothers or sisters will get the same mix, unless you are identical twins.

- **Genes make us unique**—making us tall or short, fair or dark, brilliant dancers or speakers, healthy or likely to get particular illnesses, and so on.

- **Genes are sections** of DNA—a microscopically tiny molecule inside each cell.

- **DNA** is shaped in a double helix with linking bars, like a twisted rope ladder.

- **The bars of DNA** are four special chemicals called bases: guanine, adenine, cytosine, and thymine.

- **The bases in DNA** are set in groups of three called codons, and the order of the bases in each codon varies to provide a chemical code for the cell to make a particular amino acid. The cell puts together different amino acids to make different proteins.

DNA coiled into a chromosome

"Rungs" made from four different chemical bases

DNA's double spiral shape, like a twisted rope ladder

DNA unraveling

The new copy, called RNA is used to make the proteins

Each of these bases will pair up with only one other base

Strands of DNA dividing to make a template

Chromosome in miniature

◀ DNA (Deoxyribonucleic Acid) is the amazing tiny molecule inside every cell that carries all your genes in a chemical code – the genetic code. Most of the time it is coiled up inside the chromosomes, but when needed it unravels to reveal its double helix shape. Each of the four bases that make the rungs pairs with only one other—guanine with cytosine, and adenine with thymine. So the sequence of bases along one strand of the DNA is a perfect mirror image of the sequence on the other side. When the strand temporarily divides down the middle, each strand can be used like a template to make a copy. This is how instructions are issued.

Breathing

- **You breathe** because every cell in your body needs a continuous supply of oxygen to burn glucose, the high-energy substance from digested food.

- **Scientists** call breathing "respiration." Cellular respiration is the way that cells use oxygen to burn glucose.

- **The oxygen in air** is taken into your lungs, and then carried in your blood to your body cells.

- **Waste carbon dioxide** from your cells is returned by your blood to your lungs, to be breathed out.

- **On average** you breathe in about 15 times a minute. If you run hard, the rate soars to around 80 times a minute.

- **Newborn babies** breathe about 40 times a minute.

- **If you live to the age of 80**, you will have taken well over 600 million breaths.

- **A normal breath** takes in about 0.8pt (0.4l) of air. A deep breath can take in ten times as much.

- **Your diaphragm** is a dome-shaped sheet of muscle between your chest and stomach, which works with your chest muscles to make you breathe in and out.

- **Scientists** call breathing in "inhalation," and breathing out "exhalation."

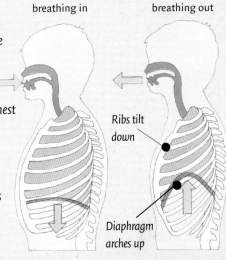

breathing in   breathing out

▶ Air is sucked in through your nose and mouth as your diaphragm pulls your lungs down and your chest muscles pull your ribs up and out. Air is forced out again when the diaphragm arches up and the rib muscles relax to allow the ribs to tilt down.

Ribs tilt down

Diaphragm arches up

Coordination

- **Coordination** means balanced or skillful movement.

- **To make you move**, your brain has to send signals out along nerves telling all the muscles involved exactly what to do.

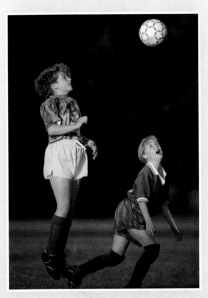

◀ Ball skills demand incredible muscle coordination. The eyes follow the ball to tell the brain exactly where it is. At the same time, the brain also relies on a high-speed stream of sensory signals from the proprioceptor cells in order to tell it exactly where the leg is, and to keep the body perfectly balanced.

- **Coordination of the muscles** is handled by the cerebellum at the back of your brain (see The brain).

- **The cerebellum** is told what to do by the brain's motor cortex (see The cortex).

- **The cerebellum sends** its commands via the basal ganglia in the middle of the brain.

- **Proprioceptor** means "one's own sensors," and proprioceptors are nerve cells that are sensitive to movement, pressure, or stretching.

- **Proprioceptors are all over your body**—in muscles, tendons, and joints—and they all send signals to your brain telling it the position or posture of every body part.

- **The hair cells** in the balance organs of your ear are also proprioceptors (see Balance).

> ★ STAR FACT ★
> Proprioceptors are what allow you to touch forefingers behind your back.

Mood

- **Mood is** your state of mind—whether you are happy or sad, angry or afraid, overjoyed, or depressed.

- **Moods and emotions** seem to be strongly linked to the structures in the center of the brain, where unconscious activities are controlled (see the brain).

- **Moods** have three elements: how you feel, what happens to your body, and what they make you do.

- **Some scientists** think the way you feel causes changes in the body—you are happy so you smile, for example.

- **Other scientists** think changes in the body alter the way you feel—smiling makes you happy.

- **Yet other scientists** think moods start automatically —before you even know it—when something triggers off a reaction in the thalamus in the center of the brain.

> ★ STAR FACT ★
> In one experiment, people injected with adrenaline found rotten jokes much funnier!

- **The thalamus** then sends mood signals to the brain's cortex and you become aware of the mood.

- **The thalamus** also sets off automatic changes in the body through nerves and hormones.

- **Certain memories or experiences** are so strongly linked in your mind that they can automatically trigger a certain mood.

▶ Scientists are only just beginning to discover how moods and emotions are linked to particular parts of the brain.

Fats

- **Fats** are an important source of energy. Along with carbohydrates and proteins, they make up your body's three main components of foods.

- **While carbohydrates** are generally used for energy immediately, your body often stores fat to use for energy in times of shortage.

- **Weight for weight**, fats contain twice as much energy as carbohydrates.

- **Fats (or lipids)** are important organic (life) substances, found in almost every living thing. They are made from substances called fatty acids and glycerol.

- **Food fats** are greasy, vegetable, or animal fats that will not dissolve in water.

- **Most vegetable fats** such as corn oil and olive oil are liquid, although some nut fats are solid.

◀ Fats are either saturated or unsaturated. Cheese is a saturated fat, which means its fatty acids are saturated with as much hydrogen as they can hold. Saturated fats are linked to high levels of the substance cholesterol in the blood and may increase certain health risks such as heart attack.

- **Most animal fats** as in meats, milk, and cheese are solid. Milk is mainly water with some solid animal fats. Most solid fats melt when warmed.

- **Fats called triglycerides** are stored around the body as adipose tissue (body fat). These act as energy stores and also insulate the body against the cold.

- **Fats called phospholipids** are used to build body cells.

- **In your stomach**, bile from your liver and enzymes from your pancreas break fats down into fatty acids and glycerol. These are absorbed into your body's lymphatic system or enter the blood.

Capillaries

- **Capillaries** are the smallest blood vessels, linking the arterioles to the venules. They are only visible under a microscope (see Circulation).

- **Capillaries** were discovered by Marcello Malphigi in 1661.

- **There are 10 billion capillaries** in your body.

- **The largest capillary** is 0.08in (0.2mm) wide—thinner than a hair.

▲ *The work done by an athlete's muscles generates a lot of heat —which the body tries to lose by opening up capillaries in the skin, turning the skin bright red.*

- **Each capillary** is about 0.02in (0.5mm) to 0.04in (1mm) long.

- **Capillary walls** are just one cell thick, so it is easy for chemicals to pass through them.

- **It is through the capillary walls** that your blood passes oxygen, food, and waste to and from each one of your body cells.

- **There are many more capillaries** in active tissues such as muscles, liver, and kidneys than there are in tendons and ligaments.

- **Capillaries** carry more blood to reach the surface when you are warm. They carry less to keep blood away from the surface and save heat when you are cold.

> ★ STAR FACT ★
> The average capillary is thinner than a hair on your head—wide enough for red blood cells to pass through one at a time.

Germs

- **Germs** are microscopic organisms that enter your body and harm it in some way.

- **The scientific word** for "germ" is "pathogen."

- **When germs** begin to multiply inside your body, you are suffering from an infectious disease.

- **An infection** that spreads throughout your body (the flu or measles, for example) is called a systemic infection.

- **An infection** that affects only a small area (such as dirt in a cut) is called a localized infection.

- **It is often the reaction** of your body's immune system to the germ that makes you feel ill.

- **Bacteria** are single-celled organisms. They are found almost everywhere in huge numbers, and they multiply rapidly.

- **Most bacteria are harmless**, but there are three harmful groups: cocci are round cells, spirilla are coil-shaped, and bacilli are rod-shaped. These harmful bacteria cause diseases such as tetanus and typhoid.

- **Viruses** can only live and multiply by taking over other cells—they cannot survive on their own. They cause diseases such as colds, the flu, mumps, and AIDS.

- **Parasites** are animals such as tapeworms that may live in or on your body, feeding on it and making you ill.

- **Fungal spores** and tiny organisms called protozoa can also cause illness.

◀ *The disease AIDS (Acquired Immune Deficiency Syndrome) is caused by a virus called HIV. This virus gets inside vital cells of the body's immune system and weakens its ability to fight against other infections.*

Motor nerves

▲ *Motor nerves fire to make muscles move to hit the ball.*

- **Motor nerves** are connected to your muscles and tell them to move.

- **Each major muscle** has many motor nerve-endings that instruct it to contract (tighten).

- **Motor nerves cross over** from one side of your body to the other at the top of your spinal cord. This means that signals from the right side of your brain go to the left side of your body, and vice versa.

- **Each motor nerve** is paired to a proprioceptor on the muscle and its tendons (see Coordination). A signal tells the brain to say whether the muscle is tensed or relaxed.

- **If the strain** on a tendon increases, the proprioceptor sends a signal to the brain. The brain adjusts the motor signals to the muscle so it contracts more or less.

- **Motor nerve signals** originate in a part of the brain called the motor cortex (see The cortex).

- **All the motor nerves** (apart from those in the head) branch out from the spinal cord.

- **The gut** has no motor nerve-endings but plenty of sense endings, so you can feel it but cannot move it consciously.

- **The throat** has motor nerve-endings but few sense endings, so you can move it but not feel it.

- **Motor neuron disease** is a disease that attacks motor nerves within the central nervous system.

Glucose

- **Glucose** is the body's energy chemical, used as the fuel in all cell activity.

- **Glucose is a kind of sugar** made by plants as they take energy from sunlight. It is common in many fruits and fruit juices, along with fructose (see Carbohydrates).

- **The body gets its glucose** from carbohydrates in food, broken down in stages in the intestine.

- **From the intestine**, glucose travels in the blood to the liver, where excess is stored in starchy glycogen.

- **For the body to work effectively**, levels of glucose in the blood (called blood sugar) must always be correct.

- **Blood sugar levels** are controlled by two hormones, glucagon and insulin, sent out by the pancreas.

- **When blood sugar is low**, the pancreas sends out glucagon, so the liver changes more glycogen to glucose.

- **When blood sugar is high**, the pancreas sends out insulin, making the liver store more glucose as glycogen.

▲ *Glucose is built from 6 carbon, 12 hydrogen, and 6 oxygen atoms.*

Inside cells, glucose may be burned for energy, stored as glycogen, or used to make triglyceride fats (see Fats).

★ STAR FACT ★
Adrenaline and other hormones from the adrenals boost blood sugar levels.

The immune system

- **The immune system** is the complicated system of defenses that your body uses to prevent or fight off attack from germs and other invaders.

- **Your body** has a variety of barriers, toxic chemicals, and booby traps to stop germs from entering it. The skin is a barrier that stops many germs from getting in, as long as it is not broken.

- **Mucus is a thick fluid** that coats vulnerable internal parts of your body such as your stomach and nose. It also acts as a lubricant (oil), making it easier to swallow.

- **Mucus lines your airways** and lungs to protect them from smoke particles as well as from germs. Your airways may fill up with mucus when you have a cold, as your body tries to minimize the invasion of airborne germs.

> ★ STAR FACT ★
> Your vulnerable eyes are protected by tears which wash away germs. Tears also contain an enzyme called lysozome which kills bacteria.

- **Itching, sneezing, coughing, and vomiting** are your body's ways of getting rid of unwelcome invaders. Small particles that get trapped in the mucus lining of your airways are wafted out by tiny hairs called cilia.

- **The body** has many specialized cells and chemicals which fight germs that get inside you.

- **Complement** is a mixture of liquid proteins in the blood which attacks bacteria.

- **Interferons** are proteins which help the body's cells to attack viruses and also stimulate killer cells (see Lymphocytes).

- **Certain white blood cells** are cytotoxic, which means they are poisonous to invaders.

- **Phagocytes** are big white blood cells that swallow up invaders and then use an enzyme to dissolve them (see Antibodies). They are drawn to the site of an infection whenever there is inflammation.

▶ The AIDS virus, HIV, attacks the body's immune cells and prevents them from coping with infections.

▼ The body's range of interior defenses against infection is amazingly complex. The various kinds of white blood cells and the antibodies they make are particularly important.

If you get a throat infection the tonsils release cells to fight it

The adenoids in the nose are one of the body's defense centers, releasing cells to fight infections

The thymus is a gland in the chest which turns ordinary white blood cells into special T-cells that fight harmful microbes

During an infection, lymph nodes may swell up with white blood cells that have swallowed up germs

The spleen not only destroys worn-out red blood cells, but also helps make antibodies and phagocytes

Lymph glands in the groin often swell up as the body fights an infection

Sebaceous glands in the skin ooze an oil that is poisonous to many bacteria

Heredity

- **Your heredity** is all the body characteristics you inherit from your parents, whether it is your mother's black hair or your father's knobbly knees.

- **Characteristics** are passed on by the genes carried on your chromosomes (see Genes, Chromosomes).

- **The basic laws** of heredity were discovered by the Austrian monk Gregor Mendel 150 years ago.

- **Your body characteristics** are a mix of two sets of instructions: one from your mother's chromosomes and the other from your father's.

- **Each characteristic** is the work of only one gene— either your mother's or your father's. This gene is said to be "expressed."

- **The gene that is not expressed** does not vanish. Instead, it stays dormant (asleep) in your chromosomes, possibly to pass on to your children.

- **A gene** that is always expressed is called the dominant gene.

- **A recessive gene** is one that loses out to a dominant gene and stays dormant.

- **A recessive gene** may be expressed when there is no competition— that is, when the genes from both of your parents are recessive.

▲ The gene for blue eyes is recessive, but if a girl gets a blue-eye gene from both of her parents, she may have blue eyes.

Fitness

- **Fitness** is about how much and what kind of physical activity you can do without getting tired or strained.

- **Fitness depends** on your strength, flexibility, and endurance (staying power).

- **One key to fitness** is cardiovascular fitness or how well your heart and lungs respond to the extra demands of exercise.

◀ Skiing is one of the most demanding of all sports, and top skiers need to be extremely fit to cope with the extra strain on their bodies.

- **One measure of cardiovascular fitness** is how quickly your pulse rate returns to normal after exercise. The fitter you are, the quicker it returns.

- **Another measure of cardiovascular fitness** is how slowly your heart beats during exercise. The fitter you are, the slower it beats.

- **Being fit** improves your physical performance.

- **Being fit** often protects against illness.

- **Being fit** can slow down the effects of aging.

- **Cardiovascular fitness** reduces the chances of getting heart disease.

- **Fitness tests** involve comparing such things as height, weight, and body fat, and measuring blood pressure and pulse rate before and after exercise. Other tests may measure how you manage a standard exercise, such as running over a fixed distance.

Heartbeat

- **The heartbeat** is the regular squeezing of the heart muscle to pump blood around the body.
- **Four heart valves** make sure blood only moves one way.
- **The heartbeat** is a sequence called the cardiac cycle and it has two phases: systole and diastole.
- **Systole** is when the heart muscle contracts (tightens). Diastole is the resting phase between contractions.
- **Systole begins** when a wave of muscle contraction sweeps across the heart and squeezes blood from each of the atria into the two ventricles.
- **When the contraction** reaches the ventricles, they squeeze blood into the arteries.
- **In diastole**, the heart muscle relaxes and the atria fill with blood again.
- **Heart muscle** on its own would contract automatically.
- **Nerve signals** make the heart beat faster or slower.

Right atrium

Left atrium

Valves open

Left ventricle

Right ventricle

Red: oxygenated blood to body

Valves open

Blue: deoxygenated blood to lungs

▲ Blood floods into the relaxed atria.

▲ The wave of contraction squeezes blood into ventricles.

▲ Blood is squeezed out the ventricles into the arteries.

▲ Blood starts to fill up the now relaxed atria again.

Blood

- **Blood** is the reddish liquid that circulates around your body. It carries oxygen and food to body cells, and takes carbon dioxide and other waste away. It fights infection, keeps you warm, and distributes chemicals that control body processes.
- **Blood is made up of** red cells, white cells, and platelets, all carried in a liquid called plasma.
- **Plasma** is 90 percent water, plus hundreds of other substances, including nutrients, hormones, and special proteins for fighting infection.
- **Blood plasma** turns milky immediately after a meal high in fats.
- **Platelets** are tiny pieces of cell that make blood clots start to form to stop bleeding.
- **Blood clots also** involve a lacy, fibrous network made from a protein called fibrin. Fibrin is set in action by a

◄ Blood contains red cells and white cells, but is mainly a watery liquid called plasma.

sequence of chemicals called factors (factors I through 8).

- **The amount of blood** in your body depends on your size. An adult who weighs 175lb (80kg) has about 10.5pt (5l) of blood. A child who is half as heavy has half as much blood.
- **A drop of blood** the size of a dot on this i contains around 5 million red cells.
- **If a blood donor** gives 1pt (0.5l) of blood, the body replaces the plasma in a few hours, but it takes a few weeks to replace the red cells.

★ STAR FACT ★
Oxygen turns blood bright red when you bleed. In your veins it can be almost brown.

The heart

- **Your heart** is the size of your fist. It is inside the middle of your chest, slightly to the left.

- **The heart is a powerful pump** made almost entirely of muscle.

- **The heart contracts** (tightens) and relaxes automatically about 70 times a minute to pump blood out through your arteries.

- **The heart has two sides** separated by a muscle wall called the septum.

- **The right side** is smaller and weaker, and it pumps blood only to the lungs.

- **The stronger left side** pumps blood around the body.

- **Each side of the heart** has two chambers. There is an atrium (plural atria) at the top where blood accumulates (builds up) from the veins, and a ventricle below which contracts to pump blood out into the arteries.

- **Each side of the heart** (left and right) ejects about a third of a cup of blood every beat.

- **There are two valves** in each side of the heart to make sure that blood flows only one way: a large one between the atrium and the ventricle, and a small one at the exit from the ventricle into the artery.

- **The coronary arteries** supply the heart. If they become clogged, the heart muscle may be short of blood and stop working. This is what happens in a heart attack.

> ★ **STAR FACT** ★
> During an average lifetime, the heart pumps
> 53 million gal (200 million l) of blood.

Pulmonary artery takes blood to the lungs to pick up oxygen

Pulmonary veins bring blood back from the lungs

Two big veins called the venae cavae bring blood low in oxygen back from the body to the right side of the heart

A large artery called the aorta sends blood rich in oxygen out to the whole body

Blood loaded with oxygen from the lungs enters the left atrium

Mitral valve between the atrium and ventricle of the left side of the heart

Blood rich in oxygen returns from the lungs

Tricuspid valve between the atrium and ventricle of the right side of the heart

Left ventricle pumps blood out to the whole body via the aorta

Septum

Right ventricle pumps blood to the lungs

◄ The heart is a remarkable double pump, with two pumping chambers, the left and the right ventricles. It contracts automatically to squeeze jets of blood out of the ventricles and through the arteries.

Pregnancy

- **Pregnancy** begins when a woman's ovum (egg cell) is fertilized by a man's sperm cell. Usually this happens after sexual intercourse, but it can begin in a laboratory.

- **When a woman becomes pregnant** her monthly menstrual periods stop. Tests on her urine show whether she is pregnant.

- **During pregnancy**, the fertilized egg divides again and again to grow rapidly—first to an embryo (the first eight weeks), and then to a fetus (from eight weeks until birth).

- **Unlike an embryo**, a fetus has grown legs and arms, as well as internal organs such as a heart.

- **Pregnancy lasts nine months**, and the time is divided into three trimesters (periods of about 12 weeks).

- **The fetus** lies cushioned in its mother's uterus (womb) in a bag of fluid called the amniotic sac.

- **The mother's blood** passes food and oxygen to the fetus via the placenta, also known as the afterbirth.

- **The umbilical cord** runs between the fetus and the placenta, carrying blood between them.

- **During pregnancy** a woman gains 30 percent more blood, and her heart rate goes up.

- **During pregnancy** a woman's breasts grow and develop milk glands.

▼ *After about 16 weeks, a pregnant woman may go for an ultrasound scan to check that the fetus is healthy.*

Muscle movement

◄ *A very high-powered electron microscope reveals purple myofibrils of myosin, each a tiny, tiny fraction in width. The orange is actin.*

★ STAR FACT ★
If all the muscles in your body pulled together, they could lift a bus.

- **Most muscles are long and thin** and they work by pulling themselves shorter, sometimes contracting by up to half their length.

- **Skeletal muscles**, the muscles that make you move, are made of special cells which have not just one nucleus like other cells do, but many nuclei in a long myofiber.

- **Muscles are made** from hundreds or thousands of these fibers bound together like fibers in string.

- **Muscle fibers** are made from tiny strands called

myofibrils, each marked with dark bands, giving the muscle its name of striped or "striated" muscle.

- **The stripes** in muscle are alternate bands of filaments of two substances: actin and myosin.

- **The actin and myosin** interlock, like teeth on a zipper.

- **When a nerve signal** comes from the brain, chemical "hooks" on the myosin twist and yank the actin filaments along, shortening the muscle.

- **The chemical hooks** on myosin are made from a stem called a cross-bridge and a head made of a chemical called adenosine triphosphate or ATP.

- **ATP is sensitive to calcium**, and the nerve signal from the brain that tells the muscle to contract does its work by releasing a flood of calcium to trigger the ATP.

Reflexes

- **Reflexes** are muscle movements that are automatic (they happen without you thinking about them).
- **Inborn reflexes** are reflexes you were born with, such as urinating or shivering when you are cold.
- **The knee-jerk** is an inborn reflex that makes your leg jerk up when the tendon below your knee is tapped.
- **Primitive reflexes** are reflexes that babies have for a few months after they are born.
- **One primitive reflex** is when you put something in a baby's hand and it automatically grips it.
- **Conditioned reflexes** are those you learn through habit, as certain pathways in the nervous system are used again and again.
- **Conditioned reflexes** help you do anything from holding a cup to playing football without thinking.
- **Reflex reactions** are what pulls your hand away from hot things before you have had time to think about it.

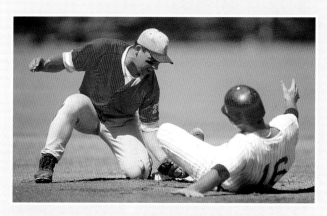

▲ *Many sportsmen rely on lightning reflexes—actions too fast for the brain to even think about.*

- **Reflex reactions** work by short-circuiting the brain. The alarm signal from your hand sets off motor signals in the spinal cord to move the hand.
- **A reflex arc** is the nerve circuit from sense to muscle via the spinal cord.

The kidneys

- **The kidneys** are a pair of bean-shaped organs inside the small of the back.
- **The kidneys** are the body's water control and blood-cleaner.
- **The kidneys** are high-speed filters that draw off water and important substances from the blood. They let unwanted waste substances go (see urine).
  - **The kidneys filter** about 2.7pt (1.3l) of blood a minute.

Outer layer, or cortex

Inner layer—medulla

Urine collects in the central area of kidney, the pelvis

◀ This cross-section diagram of a kidney shows blood entering through arteries (red) and leaving through veins (blue). Waste fluid drains through the ureter (yellow).

- **All the body's blood** flows through the kidneys every ten minutes, so blood is filtered 150 times a day.
- **The kidneys manage** to recycle or save every re-useable substance from the blood. It takes 180pt (85l) of water and other blood substances from every 2,000pt (1,000l) of blood, but only lets out 1.2pt (0.6l) as urine.
- **The kidneys** save nearly all the amino acids and glucose (see Diet) from the blood and 70 percent of the salt.
- **Blood entering each kidney** is filtered through a million or more filtration units called nephrons.
- **Each nephron** is an incredibly intricate network of little pipes called convoluted tubules, wrapped around countless tiny capilliaries. Useful blood substances are filtered into the tubules, then re-absorbed back into the blood in the capilliaries.
- **Blood enters each nephron** through a little cup called the Bowman's capsule via a bundle of capilliaries.

Puberty

- **Puberty** is the time when girls and boys mature sexually.

- **The age of puberty varies**: on average it is between 10 and 13 years for girls, and between 11 and 15 years for boys.

- **Puberty is started** by two hormones sent out by the pituitary gland (see The brain): the follicle-stimulating hormone and the luteinizing hormone.

- **During puberty, a girl** will develop breasts and grow hair under her arms and around her genitals.

- **Inside her body**, a girl's ovaries grow ten times as big and release sex hormones (see Reproduction: females).

- **The sex hormones** estrogen and progesterone spur the development of a girl's sexual organs and control her monthly menstrual cycle.

- **A year or so after puberty begins**, a girl has her

▲ In their early teens, girls go through puberty and begin to develop the sexual characteristics that will make them women.

menarche (the first menstrual period). When her periods come regularly, she is able to have a baby.

- **For a boy during puberty**, his testes grow and hair sprouts on his face, under his arms, and around his genitals. His voice also becomes lower (see Reproduction: male).

- **Inside his body**, a boy's testes begin to make sperm.

> ★ STAR FACT ★
> By the time a boy is 15, his testicles can make 200 million new sperm a day.

The lymphatic system

- **The lymphatic system** is your body's sewer, the network of pipes that drains waste from the cells.

- **The "pipes" of the lymphatic system** are called lymphatics or lymph vessels.

- **The lymphatics** are filled by a watery liquid called lymph fluid which, along with bacteria and waste chemicals, drains from body tissues such as muscles.

- **The lymphatic system** has no pump, like the heart, to make it circulate. Instead, lymphatic fluid circulates as a side effect of the heartbeat and muscle movement.

- **At places** in the lymphatic system there are tiny lumps called nodes. These are filters which trap germs that have got into the lymph fluid.

- **In the nodes**, armies of white blood cells called lymphocytes neutralize or destroy germs.

- **When you have** a cold or other infection, the lymph nodes in your neck or groin, or under your arm, may swell, as lymphocytes fight germs.

▶ The lymphatic system is a branching network of little tubes that reaches throughout the body. It drains back to the center of the body, running into branches of the superior vena cava, the body's main vein to the heart.

Concentration of lymph nodes

- **Lymph fluid** drains back into the blood via the body's main vein, the superior vena cava (see Heart).

- **The lymphatic system** is not only the lymphatics and lymph nodes, but includes the spleen, the thymus, the tonsils, and the adenoids (see Immune system).

- **On average**, at any time, about 2 to 4pt (1 to 2l) of lymph fluid circulate in the lymphatics and body tissues.

Reproduction: females

- **A girl or woman's reproductive system** is where her body stores, and nurtures the egg cells (ova – singular, ovum) that create a new human life when joined with a male sperm cell.

- **All the egg cells** are stored from birth in the ovaries: two egg-shaped glands inside the pelvic region. Each egg is stored in a tiny sac called a follicle.

- **One egg cell** is released every monthly menstrual cycle by one of the ovaries.

- **A monthly menstrual cycle starts** when FSH (follicle-stimulating hormone) is sent by the pituitary gland in the brain to spur follicles to grow.

- **As follicles grow**, they release the sex hormone estrogen. Estrogen makes the lining of the uterus (womb) thicken.

- **When an egg is ripe**, it slides down a duct called a Fallopian tube.

- **If a woman** has sexual intercourse at this time, sperm from the man's penis may swim up her vagina, enter her womb, and fertilize the egg in the Fallopian tube.

- **If the egg is fertilized**, the womb lining goes on thickening ready for pregnancy, and the egg begins to develop into an embryo.

- **If the egg is not fertilized**, it is shed with the womb lining in a flow of blood from the vagina. This shedding is called a menstrual period.

Fallopian tube
Ovary
Uterus
Cervix
Vagina

◀ This is a frontal view of the inside of a female reproductive system, showing the two ovaries and Fallopian tubes, which join to the uterus.

Lymphocytes

▲ A lymph node packed with lymphocytes fighting infection.

- **Lymphocytes** are white blood cells that play a key role in the immune system, which targets invading germs.

- **There are two kinds of lymphocyte**: B lymphocytes (B-cells) and T lymphocytes (T-cells).

- **B-cells** develop into plasma cells that make antibodies to attack bacteria such as those which cause cholera.

- **T-cells** work against viruses and other micro-organisms that hide inside body cells. T-cells help identify and destroy these invaded cells or their products. They also attack certain bacteria.

- **There are two kinds of T-cell:** killers and helpers.

- **Helper T-cells** identify invaded cells and send out chemicals called lymphokines as an alarm, telling killer T-cells to multiply.

- **Invaded cells** give themselves away by abnormal proteins on their surface.

- **Killer T-cells** lock on to the cells identified by the helpers, then move in, and destroy them.

- **Some B-cells**, called memory B-cells, stay around for a long time, ready for a further attack by the same organism.

★ STAR FACT ★
If you get the flu, it is your T lymphocytes that come to the rescue to fight off the virus.

The ear

- **Pinnae** (singular, pinna) are the ear flaps you can see on the side of your head, and they are simply collecting funnels for sounds.

- **A little way inside your head**, sounds hit a thin, tight wall of skin, called the eardrum, making it vibrate.

- **When the eardrum vibrates**, it shakes three little bones called ossicles. These are the smallest bones in the body.

- **The three ossicle bones** are the malleus (hammer), the incus (anvil), and the stapes (stirrup).

> ★ STAR FACT ★
> If your hearing is normal, you can hear sounds as deep as 20 Hertz (Hz) (vibrations per second) and as high as 20,000 Hz.

- **When the ossicles vibrate**, they rattle a tiny membrane called the oval window, intensifying the vibration.

- **The oval window** is 30 times smaller in area than the eardrum.

- **Beyond the oval window is the cochlea**—a winding collection of three, liquid-filled tubes, which looks a bit like a snail shell.

- **In the middle tube** of the cochlea there is a flap which covers row upon row of tiny hairs. This is called the organ of Corti.

- **When sounds make** the eardrum vibrate, the ossicles tap on the oval window, making pressure waves shoot through the liquid in the cochlea and wash over the flap of the organ of Corti, waving it up and down.

- **When the organ of Corti waves**, it tugs on the tiny hairs under the flap. These send signals to the brain via the auditory nerve—and you hear a sound.

▼ Most of your ear is hidden inside your head. It is an amazingly complex and delicate structure for picking up the tiny variations in air pressure created by a sound.

Liquid-filled semi-circular canals help you to balance

Hammer

Eardrum

Ear flap

Auditory nerve

Cochlea

Eustachian tube for relieving air pressure

Stirrup

Oval window

Anvil

Ear canal

Excretion

- **Digestive excretion** is the way your body gets rid of food that it cannot digest.
- **Undigested food** is prepared for excretion in your large intestine or bowel.
- **The main part** of the large intestine is the colon, which is almost as long as you are tall.
- **The colon** converts the semi-liquid "chyme" (see Digestion) of undigested food into solid waste, by absorbing water.
- **The colon** soaks up 3.2pt (1.5l) of water every day.
- **The colon walls** also absorb sodium and chlorine and get rid of bicarbonate and potassium.
- **Billions of bacteria** live inside the colon and help turn the chyme into feces. These bacteria are

◄ To work well, your bowel needs plenty of roughage, the indigestible cellulose plant fibers found in food such as beans and wholewheat bread. Roughage keeps the muscles of the bowel exercised.

harmless as long as they do not spread to the rest of the body.

- **Bacteria in the colon** make vitamins K and B—as well as smelly gases such as methane and hydrogen sulphide.
- **The muscles of the colon** break the waste food down into segments ready for excretion.

> ★ STAR FACT ★
> About a third of all feces is not old food but a mix of "friendly" gut bacteria.

Cartilage

- **Cartilage is a rubbery** substance used in various places around the body. You can feel cartilage in your ear flap if you move it back and forward.
- **Cartilage is made** from cells called chondrocytes embedded in a jello-like ground substance with fibers of collagen, all wrapped in an envelope of tough fibers.
- **There are three types**: hyaline, fibrous, and elastic.
- **Hyaline cartilage** is the most widespread in your body. It is almost clear, pearly white, and quite stiff.
- **Hyaline cartilage** is used in many of the joints between bones to cushion them against impacts.
- **Fibrous cartilage** is really tough cartilage used in between the bones of the spine and in the knee.
- **Cartilage in the knee** makes two dish shapes called menisci between the thigh and shin bones. Football players often damage these cartilages.
- **Elastic cartilage** is very flexible and used in your airways, nose, and ears.

- **Cartilage grows** quicker than bone, and the skeletons of babies in the womb are mostly cartilage, which gradually ossifies (hardens to bone).
- **Osteoarthritis** is when joint cartilage breaks down, making movements painful.

Fluid-filled sac called a bursa

Hyaline cartilage covering over end of bone

Knee cap

Fibrous cartilage of meniscus

Thigh bone

Shin bone

► No joint in your body is put under more stress than your knee. Besides ligaments and tendons to support it, it has thick cushions of cartilage.

Hormones

- **Hormones are** the body's chemical messengers, released from stores at times to trigger certain reactions in different parts of the body.

- **Most hormones** are endocrine hormones which are spread around your body in your bloodstream.

- **Each hormone** is a molecule with a certain shape that creates a certain effect on target cells.

- **Hormones are controlled** by feedback systems. This means they are only released when their store gets the right trigger—which may be a chemical in the blood or another hormone.

- **Major hormone sources** include: the pituitary gland just below the brain, the thyroid gland in the neck, the adrenal glands, the pancreas, a woman's ovaries, a man's testes.

- **The pituitary** is the source of many important hormones, including growth hormones which spur growing.

- **Adrenalin** is released by the adrenals to ready your body for action.

▲ In hairy moments, adrenalin boosts your breathing and heartbeat, makes your eyes widen and your skin sweat.

- **Endorphins and enkephalins** block or relieve pain.

- **Estrogen and progesterone** are female sex hormones that control a woman's monthly cycle.

- **Testosterone** is a male sex hormone which controls the workings of a man's sex organs.

Exercise

- **If you exercise hard,** your muscles burn energy 20 times as fast as normal, so they need much more oxygen and glucose (a kind of sugar) from the blood.

- **To boost oxygen,** your heart beats twice as fast and pumps twice as much blood, and your lungs take in ten times more air with each breath.

- **To boost glucose,** adrenalin triggers your liver to release its store of glucose.

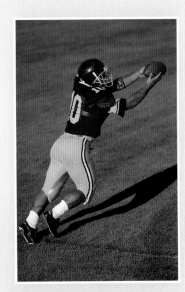

▲ A sportsman such as a football player builds up his body's ability to supply oxygen to his muscles by regular aerobic training.

- **If oxygen delivery** to muscles lags, the muscles fill up with lactic acid, affecting your body for hours afterward, and sometimes causing painful cramps.

- **The fitter you are,** the quicker your body returns to normal after exercise.

- **Aerobic exercise** is exercise that is long and hard enough for the oxygen supply to the muscles to rise enough to match the rapid burning of glucose.

- **Regular exercise** strengthens your heart building your body's ability to supply extra oxygen to your muscles.

- **Regular exercise** thickens and multiplies muscle fibers and strengthens tendons.

- **Regular exercise** can help reduce weight when it is combined with a controlled diet.

> ★ STAR FACT ★
> When you exercise hard, your body burns up energy 20 times as fast as normal.

The eye

- **Your eyes** are tough balls filled with a jello-like substance called vitreous humor.

- **The cornea** is a thin, glassy dish across the front of your eye. It allows light rays through the eye's window, the pupil, and into the lens.

- **The iris** is the colored muscular ring around the pupil. The iris narrows in bright light and widens when light is dim.

- **The lens** is just behind the pupil. It focuses the picture of the world on to the back of the eye.

- **The back of the eye** is lined with millions of light-sensitive cells. This lining is called the retina, and it registers the picture and sends signals to the brain via the optic nerve.

★ STAR FACT ★
The picture registered on your retina looks large and real—yet it is upside down and just a fraction of an inch across.

- **There are two kinds** of light-sensitive cell in the retina: rods and cones. Rods are sensitive and work in even dim light, but cannot detect colors. Cones respond to color.

- **Some kinds of cone** are very sensitive to red light, some to green, and some to blue. One theory says that the colors we see depend on how strongly they affect each of these three kinds of cone (see Color vision).

- **Each of your two eyes** gives you a slightly different view of the world. The brain combines these views to give an impression of depth and 3-D solidity.

- **Although each eye** gives a slightly different view of the world, we see things largely as just one eye sees it. This dominant eye is usually the right eye.

▼ This illustration shows your two eyeballs, with one cutaway to reveal the cornea and lens (which projects the picture of the world) and the light-sensitive retina (which registers it).

Optic chiasma in brain where signals from each eye cross over

Optic nerve which carries the signals to the brain

Retina—the lining of light-sensitive rods and cones

Tear glands and ducts

Muscles that turn the eye

Choroid (lining)

Sclera (shell)

Ligaments supporting the lens

Tear drainage duct

Pupil

Lens

Iris

Cornea

Osmosis and diffusion

▲ Like these jellyfish, every living cell must maintain the correct balance of chemicals inside and outside of them.

- **To survive**, every living cell must constantly take in the chemicals it needs and let out the ones it does not need through its thin membrane (casing). Cells do this in several ways, including osmosis, diffusion, and active transport.

- **Osmosis** is when water moves to even the balance between a weak solution and a stronger one.

- **Diffusion** is when the substances that are dissolved in water or mixed in air move to even the balance.

- **Osmosis** happens when the molecules of a dissolved substance are too big to slip through the cell membrane—only the water can move.

- **Osmosis** is vital to many body processes, including the workings of the kidneys, and the nerves.

- **Urine** gets its water from the kidneys by osmosis.

- **In diffusion**, a substance such as oxygen moves in and out of cells, while the air or water it is mixed in mainly stays put.

- **Diffusion** is vital to body processes such as cellular respiration (see Breathing), when cells take in oxygen and push out waste carbon dioxide.

- **Active transport** is the way a cell uses protein-based "pumps" or "gates" in its membrane to draw in and hold substances that might otherwise diffuse out.

- **Active transport** uses energy and is how cells draw in most of their food such as glucose.

Reproduction: male

- **A boy or man's reproductive system** is where his body creates the sperm cells that combine with a female egg cell to create a new human life.

- **Sperm cells** look like microscopically tiny tadpoles. They are made in the testes, inside the scrotum.

- **The testes and scrotum** hang outside the body where it is cooler, because this improves sperm production.

- **At 15**, a boy's testes can make 200 million sperm a day.

- **Sperm leave** the testes via the epididymis, a thin, coiled tube, about 20ft (6m) long.

- **When the penis** is stimulated during sexual intercourse, sperm are driven into a tube called the vas deferens and mix with a liquid called seminal fluid to make semen.

- **Semen** shoots through the urethra (the tube inside the penis through which males urinate) and is ejaculated into the female's vagina.

- **The male sex hormone** testosterone is also made in the testes.

- **Testosterone** stimulates bone and muscle growth.

- **Testosterone** also stimulates the development of male characteristics such as facial hair and a deeper voice.

Vas deferens — Bladder — Seminal vesicle which makes seminal fluid — Prostate gland — Epididymis — Scrotum

Erectile tissue which stiffens the penis — Urethra — Pubic bone — Penis — Testis

▶ This is a side view of the inside of a boy's reproductive organs.

Aging

▲ *Changes in health standards mean that more and more people than ever before are remaining fit in old age.*

- **Most people live** for between 60 and 100 years, although a few live even longer than this.

- **The longest officially confirmed age** is that of Frenchwoman Jeanne Calment, who died in 1997, aged 122 years and 164 days.

- **Life expectancy** is how long statistics suggest you are likely to live.

- **On average in Europe**, men can expect to live about 75 years and women about 80. However, because health is improving generally, people are living longer.

- **As adults grow older**, their bodies begin to deteriorate (fail). Senses such as hearing, sight, and taste weaken.

- **Hair goes gray** as pigment (color) cells stop working.

- **Muscles weaken** as fibers die.

- **Bones become more brittle** as they lose calcium. Cartilage shrinks between joints, causing stiffness.

- **Skin wrinkles** as the rubbery elastin and collagen fibers that support it sag. Exposure to sunlight speeds this up, which is why the face and hands get wrinkles first.

- **Circulation and breathing weaken.** Blood vessels may become stiff and clogged, forcing the heart to work harder and raising blood pressure.

Microscopes

- **Optical microscopes** use lenses and light to magnify things (make them look bigger). By combining two or more lenses, they can magnify specimens up to 2,000 times and reveal individual blood cells.

- **To magnify things more**, scientists use electron microscopes. These fire beams of tiny charged particles called electrons.

- **Electrons** have wavelengths 100,000 times smaller than light and so can give huge magnifications.

- **Scanning electron microscopes** (SEMs) are able to magnify things up to 100,000 times.

- **SEMs** show structures inside body cells.

- **Transmission electron microscopes** (TEMs) magnify even more than SEMs, up to 5 million times.

- **TEMs** can reveal the individual molecules in a cell.

- **SEM specimens** (things studied) must be coated in a special substance such as gold. They give a three-dimensional view.

- **Optical microscope specimens** are thinly sliced and placed between two glass slides.

- **Microscopes help** to identify germs.

▼ *Microscopes reveal a lot about the body.*

Ribs

- **Together,** the rib bones, breastbone, and backbone make up the rib cage.

- **The ribs** are the thin, flattish bones that curve around your chest.

- **The rib cage** protects vital organs: heart, lungs, liver, kidneys, stomach, and spleen.

▶ *The ribs provide a frame for the chest, and a protective cage around the heart, lungs, and other organs.*

Costal cartilage
Sternum (breastbone)
Lung
Heart
Stomach
True ribs
Liver
False ribs

- **You have 12 pairs** of ribs altogether.

- **Seven pairs** are called true ribs. Each rib is attached to the breastbone in front and curves around to join on to one of the vertebrae that make up the backbone, via a strip of costal cartilage.

- **There are three pairs** of false ribs, attached to vertebrae but not linked to the breastbone. Instead, each rib is attached by cartilage to the rib above it.

- **There are two pairs** of floating ribs. These are attached only to the vertebrae of the backbone.

- **The gaps between** the ribs are called intercostal spaces, and they contain thin sheets of muscle which expand and relax the chest during breathing.

- **Flail chest** is when many ribs are broken (often in a car accident) and the lungs heave the chest in and out.

The pancreas

- **The pancreas** is a large, carrot-shaped gland which lies just below and behind your stomach.

- **The larger end** of the pancreas is on the right, tucking into the gut (see Digestion). The tail end is on the left, just touching your spleen.

- **The pancreas** is made from a substance called exocrine tissue, embedded with hundreds of nests of hormone glands called the islets of Langerhans.

- **The exocrine tissue** secretes (releases) pancreatic enzymes such as amylase into the intestine to help digest food (see Enzymes).

- **Amylase** breaks down carbohydrates into simple sugars such as maltose, lactose, and sucrose.

- **The pancreatic enzymes** run into the intestine via a pipe called the pancreatic duct, which joins to the bile duct. This duct also carries bile (see The liver).

- **The pancreatic enzymes** only start working when they meet other kinds of enzyme in the intestine.

- **The pancreas** also secretes the body's own antacid, sodium bicarbonate, to settle an upset stomach.

- **The islets of Langerhans** secrete two important hormones, which are insulin and glucagon.

- **Insulin and glucagon** regulate blood sugar levels (see Glucose).

▶ *This is a microscopic view of the pancreas, with the islets of Langerhans (shown in purple) embedded in the exocrine tissue.*

Sensory nerves

- **Sensory nerves** are the nerves that carry information to your brain from sense receptors all over your body.

- **Each sense receptor** in the body is linked to the brain by a sensory nerve.

- **Most sensory nerves** feed their signals to the somatosensory cortex—the strip around the top of the brain where sensations are registered (see the cortex).

- **Massive bundles** of sensory nerve cells form the nerves that link major senses such as the eyes, ears, and nose to the brain.

- **The eyes are linked to the brain** by the optic nerves.

- **The ears are linked to the brain** by the auditory nerves.

- **The nose is linked to the brain** by the olfactory tracts.

- **In the skin**, many sense receptors are simply "free"— they are exposed sensory nerve-endings.

- **The sciatic nerve** to each leg is the longest nerve in the body. Its name is from the Latin for "pain in the thigh."

▲ *Some of our most pleasant feelings, such as being hugged or stroked, are sent to the brain by sensory nerves.*

- **We can tell** how strong a sensation is by how fast the sensory nerve fires signals to the brain. But no matter how strong the sensation is, the nerve does not go on firing at the same rate and soon slows down.

Sex hormones

▲ *A girl's sexual development depends on female sex hormones.*

- **The sexual development** of girls and boys depends on the sex hormones (see Reproduction).

- **Sex hormones** control the development of primary and secondary sexual characteristics, and regulate all sex-related processes such as sperm and egg production.

- **Primary sexual characteristics** are the development of the major sexual organs, such as the genitals.

- **Secondary sexual characteristics** are other differences between the sexes, such as men's beards.

- **There are three main types of sex hormone**: androgens, estrogens and progesterones.

- **Androgens** are male hormones such as testosterone. They make a boy's body develop features such as a beard, deepen his voice, and make his penis grow.

- **Estrogen** is the female hormone made mainly in the ovaries. It not only makes a girl develop her sexual organs, but controls her monthly menstrual cycle.

- **Progesterone** is the female hormone that prepares a girl's uterus (womb) for pregnancy every month.

- **Some contraceptive pills** have estrogen in them to prevent the ovaries from releasing their egg cells.

★ **STAR FACT** ★
Boys have female sex hormones and girls male sex hormones, but they usually have no effect.

Muscles

- **Muscles are special fibers** that contract (tighten) and relax to move parts of the body.

- **Voluntary muscles** are all the muscles you can control by will or thinking, such as your arm muscles.

- **Involuntary muscles** are the muscles you cannot control at will, but work automatically, such as the muscles that move food through your intestine.

- **Most voluntary muscles** cover the skeleton and are therefore called skeletal muscles. They are also called striated (striped) muscle because there are dark bands on the bundles of fiber that form them.

- **Most involuntary muscles** form sacs or tubes such as the intestine or the blood vessels. They are called smooth muscle as they lack the bands or stripes of voluntary muscles.

- **Heart muscle** is a unique combination of skeletal and smooth muscle. It has its own built-in contraction rhythm of 70 beats a minute, and special muscle cells that work like nerve cells for transmitting

> ★ STAR FACT ★
> The body's smallest muscle is the stapedius, inside the ear.

the signals for waves of muscle contraction to sweep through the heart.

- **Most muscles are arranged in pairs**, because although muscles can shorten themselves, they cannot forcibly make themselves longer. So the flexor muscle that bends a joint is paired with an extensor muscle to straighten it out again.

- **Your body's longest muscle** is the sartorius on the inner thigh.

- **Your body's widest muscle** is the external oblique which runs around the side of the upper body.

- **Your body's biggest muscle** is the gluteus maximus in your buttock (bottom).

▶ Under a microscope, you can see that muscles are made from bundles and bundles of tiny fibers.

▶ You have more than 640 skeletal muscles and they make up over 40 percent of your body's entire weight, covering your skeleton like a bulky blanket. The illustration here shows only the main surface muscles of the back, but your body has at least two layers, and sometimes three layers of muscle beneath its surface muscles. Most muscles are firmly anchored at both ends and attached to the bones either side of a joint, either directly or via tough fibers called tendons.

Trapezius turns head

Deltoid lifts shoulder

Triceps straighten arm

Latissimus dorsi pulls arm back and down

External oblique holds trunk straight

Gluteus maximus

Extensor digitorum straightens fingers

Anatomy

▶ Much of our basic knowledge of human anatomy comes from the anatomists of the 16th and 17th centuries, who meticulously cut up corpses and then accurately drew what they saw.

- **Anatomy** is the study of the structure of the human body.

- **Comparative anatomy** compares the structure of our bodies to those of animals' bodies.

- **The first great anatomist** was the Ancient Roman physician, Galen (AD129–199).

- **The first great book** of anatomy was written in 1543 by the Flemish scientist Andreas Vesalius (1514–1564). It is called *De Humani Corporis Fabrica* ("On the fabric [structure] of the Human Body.")

- **To describe the location** of body parts, anatomists divide the body into quarters.

- **The anatomical position** is the way the body is positioned to describe anatomical terms—upright, with the arms hanging down by the sides, and the eyes, palms, and toes facing forward.

- **The central coronal plane** divides the body into front and back halves. Coronal planes are any slice across the body from side to side, parallel to the central coronal plane.

- **The ventral or anterior** is the front half of the body.

- **The dorsal or posterior** is the back half of the body.

- **Every part of the body** has a Latin name, but anatomists use a simple English name if there is one.

Sleeping

- **When you are asleep**, many your body functions go on as normal—even your brain goes on receiving sense signals. But your body may save energy and do routine repairs.

- **Lack of sleep** can be dangerous. A newborn baby needs 18 to 20 hours sleep a day. An adult needs 7 to 8.

- **Sleep is controlled** in the brain stem (see The brain). Dreaming is stimulated by signals fired from a part of the brain stem called the pons.

- **When you are awake**, there is little pattern to the electricity created by the firing of the brain's nerve cells. But as you sleep, more regular waves appear.

- **While you are asleep**, alpha waves sweep across the brain every 0.1 seconds. Theta waves are slower.

- **For the first 90 minutes** of sleep, your sleep gets deeper and the brain waves become stronger.

- **After about 90 minutes** of sleep, your brain suddenly starts to buzz with activity, yet you are hard to wake up.

- **After 90 minutes** of sleep, your eyes begin to flicker

▲ We all shut our eyes to sleep. Other changes to the body include the pattern of the brain's activity, relaxation of skeletal muscles, and slower heartbeat and breathing.

from side to side under their lids. This is called Rapid Eye Movement (REM) sleep.

- **REM sleep** is thought to show that you are dreaming.

- **While you sleep**, ordinary deeper sleep alternates with spells of REM lasting up to half an hour.

Body salts

- **Body salts** are not simply the salt (sodium chloride) some people sprinkle on food—they are an important group of chemicals which play a vital role in your body.

- **Examples of components** in body salts include potassium, sodium, manganese, chloride, and phosphate.

- **Body salts are important** in maintaining the balance of water in the body, and on the inside and the outside of body cells.

- **The body's thirst center** is the hypothalamus (see the brain). It monitors salt levels in the blood and sends signals telling the kidneys to keep water or to let it go.

- **You gain salt** in the food you eat.

- **You can lose salt** if you sweat heavily. This can make muscles cramp, which is why people take salt tablets

> ★ STAR FACT ★
> A saline drip is salt solution dripped via a tube into the arm of a patient who has lost blood.

▶ People who live in hot countries rely on salt in their food to make up for the loss made through sweating.

in the desert or drink a weak salt solution.

- **Too much salt** in food may result in high blood pressure.

- **When dissolved in water**, the chemical elements that salt is made from split into ions—atoms or groups of atoms with either a positive or a negative electrical charge.

- **The balance** of water and salt inside and outside of body cells often depends on a balance of potassium ions entering the cell and sodium ions leaving it.

Marrow

- **Marrow** is the soft, jello-like tissue in the center of some bones.

- **Bone marrow can be red** or yellow, depending on whether it has more blood tissue or fat tissue.

- **Red bone marrow** is the body's factory, where all blood cells, apart from some white cells, are made.

- **All bone marrow** is red when you are a baby, but as you grow older, more and more turns yellow.

- **In adults**, red marrow is only found in the ends of the limbs' long bones: the breastbone, backbone, ribs, shoulder blades, pelvis, and the skull.

- **Yellow bone marrow** is a store for fat, but it

▶ Inside the tough casing of most bones is a soft, jello-like core called the marrow, which can be either red or yellow. The red marrow of particular bones is the body's blood cell factory, making 5 million new cells a day.

may turn to red marrow when you are ill.

- **All the different** kinds of blood cell start life in red marrow as one type of cell called a stem cell. Different blood cells develop as stem cells divide and re-divide.

- **Some stem cells** divide to form red blood cells and platelets.

- **Some stem cells** divide to form lymphoblasts. These divide in turn to form various different kinds of white cells: monocytes, granulocytes and lymphocytes.

- **The white cells** made in bone marrow play a key part in the body's immune system. This is why bone marrow transplants can help people with illnesses that affect their immune system.

The skeleton

Skull
(cranium)

Lower jaw
(mandible)

◄ Your skeleton is the remarkably light, but very tough framework of bones that supports your body. It is made up of more than 200 bones.

Cheekbone
(zygomatic)

Collarbone
(clavicle)

Upper arm
(humerus)

Ribs

Backbone
(vertebrae)

Ulner

Radius

Hip bone
(pelvis)

Sacrum

Thigh bone
(femur)

Kneecap
(patella)

Shinbone
(tibia)

Calf bone
(fibula)

- **Your skeleton** is a rigid framework of bones, which provides an anchor for your muscles, supports your skin and other organs, and protects vital organs.

- **An adult's skeleton has 206 bones** joined together by rubbery cartilage. Some people have extra vertebrae (the bones of the backbone, or spine).

- **A baby's skeleton has 300** or more bones, but some of these fuse (join) together as the baby grows older.

> ★ **STAR FACT** ★
> There are 26 bones in each of your hand, including the fingers and the wrist.

- **The parts of an adult skeleton** that have fused into one bone include the skull and the pelvis (see The skull). The pelvis came from fusing the ilium bones, the ischium bones, and the pubis. The ischium is the bone that you sit down on.

- **The skeleton** has two main parts: the axial skeleton and the appendicular skeleton.

- **The axial skeleton** is the 80 bones of the upper body. It includes the skull, the vertebrae of the backbone, the ribs, and the breastbone. The arm and shoulder bones are suspended from it.

- **The appendicular skeleton** is the other 126 bones— the arm and shoulder bones, and the leg and hip bones. It includes the femur (thigh bone), the body's longest bone.

- **The word skeleton** comes from the Ancient Greek word for "dry."

- **Most women and girls** have smaller and lighter skeletons than men and boys. But in women and girls, the pelvis is much wider than in men and boys. This is because the opening has to be wide enough for a baby to get through when it is born.

◄ A microscopic view of the inside of a bone shows just why the skeleton is so light and strong. Bone is actually full of holes, like a honeycomb. Its structure is provided by criss-crossing struts called trabeculae, each angled perfectly to cope with stresses and strains.

Operations

- **A surgical operation** is when a doctor cuts into or opens up a patient's body to repair or remove a diseased or injured body part.

- **An anesthetic** is a drug or gas that either sends a patient completely to sleep (a general anesthetic), or numbs part of the body (a local anesthetic).

- **Minor operations** are usually done with just a local anesthetic.

- **Major operations** such as transplants are done under a general anesthetic.

- **Major surgery** is performed by a team of people in a specially–equipped room called an operating room.

- **The surgical team** is headed by the surgeon. There is also an anesthetist to make sure the patient stays asleep, as well as surgical assistants and nurses.

- **The operating room** must be kept very clean to prevent any infection from getting into the patient's body during the operation.

▶ *Many tricky operations are now performed using miniature cameras which help the surgeon see tiny details inside the body.*

- **In microsurgery**, a microscope is used to help the surgeon work on very small body parts such as nerves or blood vessels.

- **In laser surgery**, the surgeon cuts with a laser beam instead of a scalpel. The laser seals blood vessels as it cuts, and it is used for delicate operations such as eye surgery.

- **An endoscope is** a tube-like instrument with a TV camera at one end. It can be inserted into the patient's body during an operation to look at body parts.

The arm

- **The arm is made** from three long bones, linked by a hinge joint at the elbow.

- **The two bones** of the lower arm are the radius and the ulnar.

- **The radius** supports the thumb side of the wrist.

- **The ulnar** supports the outside of the wrist.

- **The wrist** is one of the best places to test the pulse, since major arteries come nearer the surface here than at almost any other place in the body.

▶ *Look at the inside of your wrist on a warm day and you may be able to see the radial artery beneath the skin.*

Humerus

Ulnar

Radius

Ulnar artery

Radial artery

- **The two major muscles** of the upper arm are the biceps (which bends the elbow) and the triceps (which straightens it).

- **The hand is made** from 26 bones, including the carpals (wrist bones), the metacarpals (hand bones), and the phalanges (finger bones).

- **There are no strong muscles** in the hand. When you grip firmly, most of the power comes from muscles in the lower arm, linked to the bones of the hand by long tendons.

- **The shoulder** is one of the most flexible but least stable joints, since it is set in a very shallow socket. But it is supported by six major muscle groups, including the powerful deltoid (shoulder) muscle.

> ★ **STAR FACT** ★
> The upper arm bone is called the humerus or, jokingly, the funny bone.

Antibodies

- **Antibodies** are tiny proteins that make germs vulnerable to attack by white blood cells called phagocytes (see The immune system).

- **Antibodies are produced** by white blood cells derived from B lymphocytes (see Lymphocytes).

- **There are thousands** of different kinds of B-cell in the blood, each of which produces antibodies against a particular germ.

- **Normally, only a few B-cells** carry a particular antibody. But when an invading germ is detected, the correct B-cell multiplies rapidly to cause the release of floods of antibodies.

- **Invaders** are identified when your body's immune system recognizes proteins on their surface as foreign. Any foreign protein is called an antigen.

- **Your body was armed** from birth with antibodies for

◀ *Bacteria, viruses, and many other micro-organisms have antigens which spur B-cells into action to produce antibodies as this artists impression shows.*

germs it had never met. This is called innate immunity.

- **If your body comes across** a germ it has no antibodies for, it quickly makes some. It then leaves memory cells ready to be activated if the germ invades again. This is called acquired immunity.

- **Acquired immunity** means you only suffer once from some infections, such as chickenpox. This is also how vaccination works.

- **Allergies** are sensitive reactions that happen in your body when too many antibodies are produced, or when they are produced to attack harmless antigens.

- **Autoimmune diseases** are ones in which the body forms antibodies against its own tissue cells.

Blood cells

- **Your blood has two main kinds of cell**: red cells and white cells, plus pieces of cell called platelets (see Blood).

- **Red cells** are button-shaped and they contain mainly a red protein called hemoglobin.

- **Hemoglobin** is what allows red blood cells to ferry oxygen around your body.

- **Red cells** also contain enzymes which the body uses to

> **! NEWS FLASH !**
> Each red blood cell contains more than 200 million molecules of hemoglobin.

make certain chemical processes happen (see Enzymes).

- **White blood cells** are big cells called leucocytes and most types are involved in fighting infections.

- **Most white cells** contain tiny little grains and are called granulocytes.

- **Most granulocytes** are giant white cells called neutrophils. They are the blood's cleaners, and their task is to eat up invaders.

- **Eosinophils and basophils** are granulocytes that are involved in allergy or fighting disease. Some release antibodies that help fight infection. (Lymphocytes are also types of white cells (see Lymphocytes and Antibodies).)

Red blood cells

Granulocyte

Eosinophil

Basophil

Platelets

◀ *These are some important kinds of cell in the blood: red cells, three kinds of white cells, and platelets.*

Body systems

- **Your body systems** are interlinked—each has its own task, but they are all inter-dependent.

  - **The skeleton** supports the body, protects the major organs, and provides an anchor for the muscles.

  - **The skeletal muscles** are the ones that let you move. (Muscles are also involved in other systems.)

  - **The nervous system** is the brain and the nerves—the body's control and communications network.

  - **The digestive system** breaks down food into chemicals that the body can use.

  - **The immune system** is the body's defense against germs. It includes white blood

  ◄ *The cardiovascular system is the heart and the blood circulation. It keeps the body cells supplied with food and oxygen, and defends them against germs.*

cells, antibodies, and the lymphatic system (which circulates lymph fluid and drains away cell waste).

- **The urinary system** controls the body's water balance, removing extra water as urine and getting rid of impurities in the blood.

- **The respiratory system** takes air into the lungs to supply oxygen, and lets out waste carbon dioxide.

- **The reproductive system** is the smallest of all the systems. It is basically the sexual organs that enable people to have children. It is the only system that is different between men and women.

- **The other body systems** are the hormonal system (controling growth and coordination, intergumentary system (skin, hair, and nails), and the sensory system.

Transplants

- **More and more body parts** can now be replaced, either by transplants (parts taken from other people or animals) or by implants (artificial parts).

- **Common transplants** include the kidney, the cornea of the eye, the heart, the lung, the liver, and the pancreas.

- **Some transplant organs** (such as heart, lungs, and liver) are taken from someone who has died.

- **Other transplants** (such as kidney) may be taken from living donors.

▶ *These are just some of the artificial implants now put in place—hip, knee, shoulder, and elbow. Old people often need implants to replace joints that have deteriorated.*

- **After the transplant organ** is taken from the donor, it is washed in an oxygenated liquid and cooled to preserve it.

- **One problem** with transplants is that the body's immune system identifies the transplant as foreign and attacks it. This is called rejection.

- **To decrease** the chance of rejection, patients may be given drug such as cyclosporin to suppress their immune system.

- **Heart transplant** operations last 4 hours.

- **During a heart transplant**, the patient is connected to a heart-lung machine which takes over the heart's normal functions.

Pulse

- **Your pulse** is the powerful high-pressure surge or wave that runs through your blood and vessels as the heart contracts strongly with each beat.

- **You can feel your pulse** by pressing two fingertips on the inside of your wrist where the radial artery nears the surface (see The arm).

- **Other pulse points** include the carotid artery in the neck and the brachial artery inside the elbow.

- **Checking the pulse** is a good way of finding out how healthy someone is, which is why doctors do it.

- **Normal pulse rates** vary between 50 and 100 beats a minute. The average for a man is about 71, for a woman it is 80, and for children it is about 85.

- **Tachycardia** is the medical word for an abnormally fast heartbeat rate.

- **Someone who has tachycardia** when sitting down may have drunk too much coffee or tea, or taken drugs, or be suffering from anxiety, fever, or heart disease.

▲ By monitoring how much heart rate goes up and down during exercise, an ECG can show how healthy someone's heart is.

- **Bradycardia** is an abnormally slow heartbeat rate.

- **Arrhythmia** is an abnormality in a heartbeat rate.

- **Someone with a heart problem** may be connected to a machine called an electrocardiogram (ECG) to monitor (watch) their heartbeat.

Urine

- **Urine** is one of your body's ways of getting rid of waste (see Water).

- **Your kidneys** produce urine, filtering it from your blood.

- **Urine runs from** each kidney down a long tube called the ureter, to a bag called the bladder.

- **Your bladder fills** up with urine over several hours. When it is full, you feel the need to urinate.

▲ Doctors can get clues to illnesses by testing what substances there are in urine. Diabetes, for instance, is shown up by the presence of glucose in the urine.

- **Urine is mostly water**, but there are substances dissolved in it. These include urea, various salts, creatinine, ammonia, and blood wastes.

- **Urea** is a substance that is left after the breakdown of amino acids (see Diet).

- **Urine gets its smell** from substances such as ammonia.

- **Urine gets its color** from a yellowish blood waste called urochrome. Urochrome is left after proteins are broken down.

- **If you sweat a lot**, perhaps during a fever, your kidneys will let less water go and your urine will be stronger in color.

★ STAR FACT ★
You will urinate 12,000gal(45,000l) in your life—enough to fill a small swimming pool!

Cells

- **Cells** are the basic building blocks of your body. Most are so tiny you would need 10,000 to cover a pinhead.

- **There are over 200 different kinds** of cell in your body, including nerve cells, skin cells, blood cells, bone cells, fat cells, muscle cells, and many more.

- **A cell is basically** a little package of organic (life) chemicals with a thin membrane (casing) of protein and fat. The membrane holds the cell together, but lets nutrients in and waste out.

- **Inside the cell** is a liquid called cytoplasm, and floating in this are various minute structures called organelles.

- **At the center** of the cell is the nucleus—this is the cell's control center and it contains the amazing molecule DNA (see genes). DNA not only has all the instructions the cell needs to function, but also has the pattern for new human life.

> ★ STAR FACT ★
> There are 75 trillion cells in your body!

- **Each cell** is a dynamic chemical factory, and the cell's team of organelles is continually busy—ferrying chemicals back and forth, breaking up unwanted chemicals, and putting together new ones.

- **The biggest cells** in the body can be nerve cells. Although the main nucleus of nerve cells is microscopic, the tails of some cells can extend for a yard (metre) or more through the body, and be seen even without a microscope.

- **Among the smallest cells** in the body are red blood cells. These are just 0.0003in (0.0075mm) across and have no nucleus—their only task is ferrying oxygen.

- **Most body cells** live a very short time and are continually being replaced by new ones. The main exceptions are nerve cells—these are long-lived, but rarely replaced.

Mitochondria are the cell's power stations, turning chemical fuel supplied by the blood as glucose into energy packs of the chemical ATP (see Muscle movement)

The endoplasmic reticulum is the cell's main chemical factory, where proteins are built under instruction from the nucleus

The ribosomes are the individual chemical assembly lines, where proteins are put together from basic chemicals called amino acids (see Diet)

The nucleus is the cell's control center, sending out instructions via a chemical called messenger RNA whenever a new chemical is needed

The lysosomes are the cell's garbage cans, breaking up any unwanted material

The Golgi bodies are the cell's despatch center, where chemicals are bagged up inside tiny membranes to send where they are needed

◀ This illustration shows a typical cell, cutaway to show some of the different organelles (special parts of a cell) that keep it working properly. The instructions come from the nucleus in the cell's control center, but every kind of organelle has its own task.

Skin

- **Skin is your protective coat**, shielding your body from the weather and from infection, and helping to keep it at just the right temperature.

- **Skin is your largest sense receptor**, responding to touch, pressure, heat, and cold (see touch).

- **Skin makes** vitamin D for your body from sunlight.

- **The epidermis** (the thin outer layer) is just dead cells.

- **The epidermis is made mainly of** a tough protein called keratin—the remains of skin cells that die off.

- **Below the epidermis** is a thick layer of living cells called the dermis, which contains the sweat glands.

- **Hair roots** have tiny muscles that pull the hair upright when you are cold, giving you goose bumps.

> ★ STAR FACT ★
> Your skin's thickness averages just 0.8in (2mm), but it gets an eighth of all your blood supply.

- **Skin is 0.02in (0.05mm) thick** on the soles of your feet, and just 0.1in thick on your eyelids.

- **The epidermis** contains cells that make the dark pigment melanin—this gives dark-skinned people their color and fair-skinned people a tan.

▶ This is a cross-section of skin, hugely magnified, showing its key components.

Gland making oily sebum to waterproof hair

Sweat gland

Keratin layer

Epidermis

Basal layer, where new cells grow

Hair erector muscle

Dermis

Hair follicle (root)

Temperature

▶ Sweating from the sweat glands (see right) in the skin keeps you cool—not only by letting warm water out of your body, but also because as the moisture evaporates it cools your skin.

- **The inside of your body** stays at a constant temperature of 98°F (37°C), rising a few degrees only when you are ill.

- **Your body creates heat** by burning food in its cells, especially the "energy sugar" glucose.

- **Even when you are resting**, your body generates so much heat that you are comfortable only when the air is slightly cooler than you are.

- **When you are working hard**, your muscles can generate as much heat as a typical room heater.

- **Your body loses heat** as you breathe in cool air and breathe out warm air. Your body also loses heat by giving it off from your skin.

- **The body's temperature control** is the tiny hypothalamus in the lower front of the brain.

- **Temperature sensors** in the skin, in the body's core, and in the blood by the hypothalamus tell the hypothalamus how hot or cold your body is.

- **If it is too hot**, the hypothalamus sends signals to your skin telling it to sweat more. Signals also tell blood vessels in the skin to widen—this increases the blood flow, increasing the heat loss from your blood.

- **If it is too cold**, the hypothalamus sends signals to the skin to cut back skin blood flow, as well as signals to tell the muscles to generate heat by shivering.

- **If it is too cold**, the hypothalamus may also stimulate the thyroid gland to send out hormones to make your cells burn energy faster and so make more heat.

Drugs

▲ *Thousands of different drugs are today used to treat illness.*

- **Antibiotic drugs** are used to treat bacterial infections such as tuberculosis (TB) or tetanus. They were once grown as molds (fungi) but are now made artificially.

- **Penicillin** was the first antibiotic drug, discovered in a mold in 1928 by Alexander Fleming (1881–1955).

- **Analgesic drugs** such as aspirin relieve pain, mainly by stopping the body making prostaglandin, the chemical that sends pain signals to the brain.

- **Tranquillizers** are drugs that calm. Minor tranquillizers are drugs such as prozac, used to relieve anxiety.

- **Major tranquillizers** are used to treat mental illnesses such as schizophrenia.

- **Psychoactive drugs** are drugs that change your mood. Many, including heroin, are dangerous and illegal.

- **Stimulants** are drugs that boost the release of the nerve transmitter noradrenaline, making you more lively and awake. They include the caffeine in coffee.

- **Narcotics** are powerful painkillers such as morphine that mimic the body's own natural painkiller endorphin.

- **Depressants** are drugs such as alcohol which do not depress you, but instead slow down the nervous system.

> **! NEWS FLASH !**
> In future, more drugs may be made by microbes or animals with altered genes. Insulin is already made in the pancreas of pigs.

Synapses

- **Synapses** are the very tiny gaps between nerve cells.

- **When a nerve signal** goes from one nerve cell to another, it must be transmitted (sent) across the synapse by special chemicals called neurotransmitters.

- **Droplets of neurotransmitter** are released into the synapse whenever a nerve signal arrives.

- **As the droplets of neurotransmitter** lock on to the receiving nerve's receptors, they fire the signal onward.

- **Each receptor site** on a nerve-ending only reacts to certain neurotransmitters. Others have no effect.

- **Sometimes** several signals must arrive before enough neurotransmitter is released to fire the receiving nerve.

- **More than 40 neurotransmitter chemicals** have been identified.

- **Dopamine** is a neurotransmitter that works in the parts of the brain that control movement and learning. Parkinson's disease may develop when the nerves that produce dopamine break down.

- **Serotonin** is a neurotransmitter that is linked to sleeping and waking up, and also to your mood.

- **Acetylcholine** is a neurotransmitter that may be involved in memory, and also in the nerves that control muscle movement.

▶ *Nerve signals are transmitted across a synapse as chemical messengers called neurotransmitters. These lock on to receptors on the receiving nerve.*

Sending nerve

Vesicles that store neuro transmitter

Neurotransmitter chemicals

Receptor sites

Synapse (gap)

Receiving nerve

The nervous system

Brain

Cranial nerves

Spinal cord

Brachial "plexus" (nerve junction)

Ulnar nerve

Lateral pectoral nerve

Lumbar nerves

Sacral nerves

Radial nerve

Peroneal nerve

Femoral nerve

Sciatic nerve

Lateral plantar nerve

▶ The nervous system is an incredibly intricate network of nerves linking your brain to every part of the body. The nerves of the peripheral nervous system branch out to every limb and body part from the central nervous system (the brain and spinal cord).

▶ A human being has a nervous system with about 60 billion nerve cells. A spider has about 100,000.

- **The nervous system** is your body's control and communication system, made up of nerves and the brain. Nerves are your body's hot-lines, carrying instant messages from the brain to every organ and muscle—and sending back an endless stream of data to the brain about what is going on both inside and outside your body.

- **The central nervous system** (CNS) is the brain and spinal cord (see central nervous system).

- **The peripheral nervous system** (PNS) is made up of the nerves that branch out from the CNS to the rest of the body.

- **The main branches of the PNS** are the 12 cranial nerves in the head, and the 31 pairs of spinal nerves that branch off the spinal cord.

- **The nerves of the PNS** are made up of long bundles of nerve fibers, which in turn are made from the long axons (tails) of nerve cells, bound together like the wires in a telephone cable.

- **In many places**, sensory nerves (which carry sense signals from the body to the brain) run alongside motor nerves (which carry the brain's commands telling muscles to move).

- **Some PNS nerves** are as wide as your thumb. The longest is the sciatic, which runs from the base of the spine to the knee.

- **The autonomic nervous system** (ANS) is the body's third nervous system. It controls all internal body processes such as breathing automatically, without you even being aware of it.

- **The ANS** is split into two complementary (balancing) parts: the sympathetic and the parasympathetic. The sympathetic system speeds up body processes when they need to be more active such as when the body is exercising or under stress. The parasympathetic slows them down.

★ **STAR FACT** ★

Millions of nerve signals enter your brain every single second of your life.

Valves

- **Valves play** a crucial part in the circulation of your blood and lymph fluid (see The lymphatic system), ensuring that liquids flow only one way.

- **The heart has four valves** to make sure blood flows only one way through it.

- **On each side of the heart** there is a large valve between the atrium and the ventricle, and a smaller one where the arteries leave the ventricle.

- **The mitral valve** is the large valve on the left. The tricuspid is the large valve on the right.

- **The aortic valve** is the smaller valve on the left. The pulmonary is the smaller valve on the right.

- **Heart valves** can sometimes get blocked, making the heart work harder or leak. Both cause what a doctor using a stethoscope hears as a heart murmur.

- **The mitral** is the valve most likely to give problems, causing an illness called mitral stenosis.

- **A faulty heart valve** may be replaced with a valve

▲ Heart valve problems may arise if the blood supply to the heart is impaired—something that may show up on an angiogram like this.

from a human or pig heart, or a mechanical valve.

- **Valves in the arteries and veins** are simply flaps that open only when the blood is flowing one way.

- **The lymphatic system** also has its own small valves to ensure lymph is squeezed only one way.

The skull

► An X-ray of the skull shows the cranial cavity which holds the brain. This is an old skull: the bright white bits are wires and clamps holding it together.

- **The skull** or cranium is the hard, bone case that protects your brain.

- **The skull looks** as though it is a single bone. In fact, it is made up of 22 separate bones, cemented together along rigid joints called sutures.

- **The dome on top** is called the cranial vault and it is made from eight curved pieces of bone fused (joined) together.

- **As well as the sinuses** of the nose (see Airways), the

skull has four large cavities—the cranial cavity for the brain, the nasal cavity (the nose), and two orbits for the eyes.

- **There are holes in the skull** to allow blood vessels and nerves through, including the optic nerves to the eyes and the olfactory tracts to the nose.

- **The biggest hole** is in the base. It is called the foramen magnum, and the brain stem goes through it to meet the spinal cord.

- **In the 19th century**, people called phrenologists thought they could figure out people's characters from little bumps on their skulls.

- **Archeologists** can reconstruct faces from the past using computer analysis of ancient skulls.

> ★ STAR FACT ★
> A baby has soft spots called fontanelles in its skull because the bones join slowly over about 18 months.

Hair

- **Humans are one of** very few land mammals to have almost bare skin. But even humans have soft, downy hair all over, with thicker hair in places.
- **Lanugo** is the very fine hair babies are covered in when they are inside the womb, from the fourth month of pregnancy onward.
- **Vellus hair** is fine, downy hair that grows all over your body until you reach puberty.
- **Terminal hair** is the coarser hair on your head, as well as the hair that grows on men's chins and around an adult's genitals.
- **The color of your hair** depends on how much there are of pigments called melanin and carotene in the hairs.
- **Hair is red or auburn** if it contains carotene.

◀ *The color of your hair depends upon melanin made in melanocytes at the root.*

- **Black, brown, and blonde hair** get their color from black melanin.
- **Each hair** is rooted in a pit called the hair follicle. The hair is held in place by its club-shaped tip, the bulb.
- **Hair grows** as cells fill with a material called keratin and die, and pile up inside the follicle.
- **The average person** has 120,000 head hairs and each grows about 0.1in (3mm) per week.

> ★ **STAR FACT** ★
> Hair in poor condition is said to be lifeless. In fact, all hair is lifeless since it is made of keratin, the material left by dead cells.

Balance

▲ *This gymnast's body is feeding her brain information continually about its position to help her stay perfectly balanced.*

- **To stay upright**, your body must send a continual stream of data about its position to your brain—and your brain must continually tell your body how to move to keep its balance.

- **Balance** is controlled in many parts of the brain including the cerebellum.
- **Your brain** learns about your body position from many sources, including: eyes, proprioceptors around the body, and the semicircular canals in the inner ear.
- **Proprioceptors** are sense receptors in your skin, muscles, and joints (see Coordination).
- **The semicircular canals** are three, tiny, fluid-filled loops in your inner ear (see The ear).
- **Two chambers** called the utricle and saccule are linked to the semicircular canals and other chambers.
- **When you move your head**, the fluid in the canals and cavities lags a little, pulling on hair detectors which tell your brain what is happening.
- **The canals** tell you whether you are nodding or shaking your head, and which way you are moving.
- **The utricle and saccule** tell you if you tilt your head.

Color vision

- **Seeing in color** depends on eye cells called cones.

- **Cones do not** work well in low light, which is why things seem gray at dusk.

- **Some cones** are more sensitive to red light, some are more sensitive to green, and some to blue.

- **The old trichromatic theory** said that you see colors by comparing the strength of the signals from each of the three kinds of cone: red, green, and blue.

- **Trichromatic theory** does not explain colors such as gold, silver, and brown.

- **The opponent-process theory** said that you see colors in opposing pairs—blue and yellow, red, and green.

- **In opponent-process theory,** lots of blue light is thought to cut your awareness of yellow, and vice versa. Lots of green cuts your awareness of red, and vice versa.

- **Now scientists** combine these theories and think that color signals from the three kinds of cone are further processed in the brain in terms of the opposing pairs.

- **Ultraviolet light** is light waves too short for you to see, although some birds and insects can see it.

◄ Seeing all the colors of the world around you depends on the color-sensitive cone cells inside your eyes.

Enzymes

- **Enzymes are** molecules, mostly protein, which alter the speed of chemical reactions in living things.

- **There are thousands of enzymes** in your body—it could not function without them.

- **Some enzymes** need an extra substance, called a coenzyme, to work. Many coenzymes are vitamins.

- **Most enzymes** have names ending in "ase," such as lygase, protease, and lipase.

- **Pacemaker enzymes** play a vital role in controlling your metabolism—the rate your body uses energy.

- **One of the most important enzyme groups** is that of the messenger RNAs, which are used as communicators by the nuclei of body cells (see Cells).

- **Many enzymes** are essential for the digestion of food, including lipase, protease, amylase, and the peptidases. Many of these are made in the pancreas.

- **Lipase** is released mainly from the pancreas into the alimentary canal (gut) to help break down fat.

- **Amylase** breaks down starches such as those in bread and fruit into simple sugars (see Carbohydrates). There is amylase in saliva and in the stomach.

- **In the gut**, the sugars maltose, sucrose, and lactose are broken down by maltase, sucrase, and lactase.

▼ After you eat a meal, a complex series of enzymes gets to work, breaking the food down into the simple molecules that can be absorbed into your blood.

Tissue and organs

- **A tissue is a body substance** made from many of the same type of cell. Muscle cells make muscle tissue, nerve cells form nerve tissue, and so on.

- **As well as cells**, some tissues include other materials.

- **Connective tissues** are made from particular cells (such as fibroblasts), plus two other materials: long fibers of protein (such as collagen) and a matrix. Matrix is a material in which the cells and fibers are set like the chocolate chips in a cookie.

- **Connective tissue** holds all the other kinds of tissue together in various ways. The adipose tissue that makes fat, tendons, and cartilage is connective tissue.

- **Bone and blood** are both connective tissues.

- **Epithelial tissue** is good lining or covering material,

▶ Lungs are largely made from special lung tissues (see right), but the mucous membrane that lines the airways is epithelial tissue.

making skin and other parts of the body.

- **Epithelial tissue** may combine three kinds of cell to make a thin waterproof layer: squamous (flat), cuboid (box-like), and columnar (pillar-like) cells.

- **Nerve tissue** is made mostly from neurons (nerve cells), plus the Schwann cells that coat them.

- **Organs** are made from combinations of tissues. The heart is made mostly of muscle tissue, but also includes epithelial, and connective tissue.

> ★ STAR FACT ★
> All your body is made from tissue and tissue fluid (liquid that fills the space between cells).

Touch

▲ As we grow up, we gradually learn to identify more and more things instantly through touch.

- **Touch or physical contact** is just one of the sensations that are spread all over your body in your skin. The others include pressure, pain, hot, and cold.

- **There are sense receptors** everywhere in your skin, but places like your face have more than your back.

- **There are 200,000** hot and cold receptors in your

skin, plus 500,000 touch and pressure receptors, and nearly 3 million pain receptors.

- **Free nerve-endings** are sort of like the bare end of a wire. They respond to all five kinds of skin sensation and are almost everywhere in your skin.

- **There are specialized receptors** in certain places, each named after their discoverer.

- **Pacini's corpuscles** and Meissner's endings react instantly to sudden pressure.

- **Krause's bulbs**, Merkel's disks, and Ruffini's endings respond to steady pressure.

- **Krause's bulbs** are also sensitive to cold.

- **Ruffini's endings** also react to changes in temperature.

> ★ STAR FACT ★
> Your brain knows just how hard you are touched from how fast nerve signals arrive.

The vocal cords

- **Speaking and singing** depend on the larynx (voice-box) in your neck (see Airways).

- **The larynx** has bands of stretchy fibrous tissue, the vocal cords, which vibrate as you breathe air out over them.

- **When you are silent**, the vocal cords are relaxed and apart, and air passes between freely.

- **When you speak or sing**, the vocal cords tighten across the airway and vibrate to make sounds.

- **The tighter** the vocal cords are stretched, the higher-pitched sounds you make.

- **The basic sound** produced by the vocal cords is a simple "aah." But by changing the shape of your mouth, lips, and especially your tongue, you can change this simple sound into letters and words.

- **Babies' vocal cords** are just 0.3in (6mm) long.

- **Women's vocal cords** are about 0.8in (20mm) long.

- **Men's vocal cords** are about 1.2in (30mm) long.

Because men's cords are longer than women's, they vibrate more slowly and give men deeper voices.

- **Boys' vocal cords** are the same length as girls' until they are teenagers—when they grow longer, making a boy's voice "break" and get deeper.

Pharynx (throat)

Epiglottis (a fold of cartilage) blocks the airway as you swallow food

Vocal cords

Trachea (windpipe) to the lungs

Esophagus to the stomach

▶ This shows a cross-section of your mouth, nose and throat, with the vocal cords at the top of the trachea.

X-rays

◀ An X-ray gives a clear picture of the inside of the chest, showing the ribs, the spine, and the branching airways in the lung. Any lung problems and blockages show up as white shadows.

- **X-rays** are a form of electromagnetic radiation, as are radio waves, microwaves, visible light, and ultraviolet. They all travel as waves, but have different wavelengths.

- **X-ray waves** are much shorter and more energetic than visible light waves. X-rays are invisible because their waves are too short for our eyes to see.

- **X-rays are made** when negatively charged particles called electrons are fired at a heavy plate made of the metal tungsten. The plate bounces back X-rays.

- **Even though they are invisible** to our eyes, X-rays register on photographic film.

- **X-rays are so energetic** that they pass through some body tissues like a light through a net curtain.

- **To make an X-ray photograph**, X-rays are shone through the body. The X-rays pass through some tissues and turn the film black, but are blocked by others, leaving white shadows on the film.

- **Each kind of tissue** lets X-rays through differently. Bones are dense and contain calcium, so they block X-rays and show up white on film. Skin, fat, muscle, and blood let X-rays through and show up black on film.

- **X-ray radiation** is dangerous in high doses, so the beam is encased in lead, and the radiographer who takes the X-ray picture stands behind a screen.

- **X-rays are** very good at showing up bone defects. So if you break a bone, it will be probably be X-rayed.

- **X-rays also** reveal chest and heart problems.

Scans

- **Diagnostic imaging** means using all kinds of complex machinery to make pictures or images of the body to help diagnose and understand a problem.

- **Many imaging techniques** are called scans, because they involve scanning a beam around the patient, in waves.

- **CT scans** rotate an X-ray beam around the patient while moving him or her slowly forward. This gives a set of pictures showing different slices of the patient.

- **CT** stands for computerized tomography.

- **MRI scans** surround the patient with such a strong magnet that all the body's protons (tiny atomic particles) turn the same way. A radio pulse is then used to knock the protons in and out of line, sending out radio signals that the scanner picks up to give the picture.

▲ *One of a series of CT scans of the head and brain.*

- **MRI** stands for magnetic resonance imaging.

- **PET scans** involve injecting the patient with a mildly radioactive substance, which flows around with the blood and can be detected because it emits (gives out) particles called positrons.

- **PET** stands for positron emission tomography.

- **PET scans** are good for seeing how blood flow alters to a particular body part.

> ★ STAR FACT ★
> PET scans allow scientists to track blood through a live brain and see which areas are in action.

Backbone

- **The backbone** (or spine) extends from the base of the skull down to the hips.

- **The backbone is not a single bone**, but a column of drum-shaped bones called vertebrae (singular, vertebra).

- **There are 33 vertebrae** altogether, although some of these fuse or join as the body grows.

- **Each vertebra** is linked to the next by small facet joints, like tiny ball-and-socket joints.

- **The vertebrae are separated** by disks of rubbery material called cartilage. These cushion the bones when you run and jump.

- **The bones of the spine** are divided into five groups from top to bottom. These are the cervical (7 bones), the thoracic (12 bones), the lumbar

◀ *The backbone is not straight—instead, its 33 vertebrae curve into an S-shape.*

(5 bones), the sacrum (5 bones fused together), and the coccyx (4 bones fused together).

- **The cervical spine** is the vertebrae of the neck. The thoracic spine is the back of the chest, and each bone has a pair of ribs attached to it. The lumbar spine is the small of the back.

- **A normal spine** curves in an S-shape, with the cervical spine curving forward, the thoracic section curving backward, the lumbar forward, and the sacrum backward.

- **On the back** of each vertebra is a bridge called the spinal process. The bridges on each bone link together to form a tube which holds the spinal cord, the body's central bundle of nerves.

> ★ STAR FACT ★
> The story character the Hunchback of Notre Dame suffered from kyphosis— excessive curving of the spine.

Arteries

- **Arteries** are blood vessels that carry blood away from the heart.
- **Systematic arteries deliver oxygenated blood** around the body. Pulmonary arteries deliver deoxygenated blood to the lungs.
- **An arteriole** is a smaller branch off an artery.
- **Arterioles branch** into microscopic capillaries.
- **Blood flows through** arteries at 11in/sec (30cm/sec) in the main artery, to 0.8in/sec (2cm/sec) in the arterioles.
- **Arteries run alongside** most of the veins that return blood to the heart.
- **The walls of arteries** are muscular and can expand or relax to control the blood flow.
- **Arteries have** thicker, stronger walls than veins, and the pressure of the blood in them is a lot higher.
- **Over-thickening of the artery walls** may be one of the causes of hypertension (high blood pressure).
- **In old age** the artery walls can harden. This is called arteriosclerosis, and can cut blood flow to the brain.

★ STAR FACT ★
Blood in an artery moves in a fast, pulsing way, while blood in a vein oozes slowly.

▶ This illustration shows how the main kinds of blood vessel in the body are connected. The artery (red) branches into tiny capillaries, which join up to supply the vein (blue).

Capillaries
Vein
Venule
Arteriole
Artery
Space within for blood
Endothelium (inner lining)
Thick muscle layer
Outer sheath

Memory

- **When you remember** something, your brain probably stores it by creating new nerve connections.
- **You have** three types of memory: sensory, short-term, and long-term.
- **Sensory memory** is when you go on feeling a sensation for a moment after it stops.
- **Short-term memory** is when the brain stores things for a few seconds, like a phone number you remember long enough to press buttons.

▲ Learning to play the violin involves non-declarative memory, in which nerve pathways become reinforced by repeated use. This is why practicing is so important.

- **Long-term memory** is memory that can last for months or maybe even your whole life.
- **Your brain** seems to have two ways of remembering things for the long term. Scientists call these declarative and non-declarative memories.
- **Non-declarative memories** are skills you teach yourself by practicing, such as playing badminton or the flute. Repetition establishes nerve pathways.
- **Declarative memories** are either episodic or semantic. Each may be sent by the hippocampus region of the brain to the correct place in the cortex, the brain's wrinkly outer layer where you do most of your thinking.
- **Episodic memories** are memories of striking events in your life, such as breaking your leg or your first day at a new school. You not only recall facts, but sensations.
- **Semantic memories** are facts such as dates. The brain seems to store these in the left temporal lobe, at the front left–hand side of your brain.

INDEX

Acknowledgments

Artist: Mike Saunders

The publishers would like to thank the following sources for the photographs used in this book:

Page 46 (B) Science Photo Library; Page 50 (T/R) The Stock Market; Page 55 (T/R) The Stock Market.

All other photographs are from MKP Archives